SOFTBALL RULES IN PICTURES

G. Jacobs McCrory

Revised and Illustrated by Michael Brown

A Perigee Book

Perigee Books
are published by
The Putnam Publishing Group
200 Madison Avenue
New York, NY 10016

Library of Congress Cataloging-in-Publication Data

Jacobs, A. G. (A. Gertrude)
    Softball rules in pictures / G. Jacobs McCrory; revised and illustrated by Michael Brown
            p.   cm.
        ISBN 0-399-51728-6
        1. Softball—Rules—Juvenile literature.   [1. Softball—Rules.]
I. Brown, Michael, 1955–   . II. Title.
GV881.2J33 1992   91-32175 CIP AC
796.357'8—dc20

Previous editions (by G. Jacobs McCrory) 1959, 1974, 1976, 1978, 1987.

The Official Softball Playing Rules reprinted by permission of the Amateur Softball Association of America

Front cover photograph courtesy of the Amateur Softball Association of America

Printed in the United States of America
        4 5 6 7 8 9 10

Contents

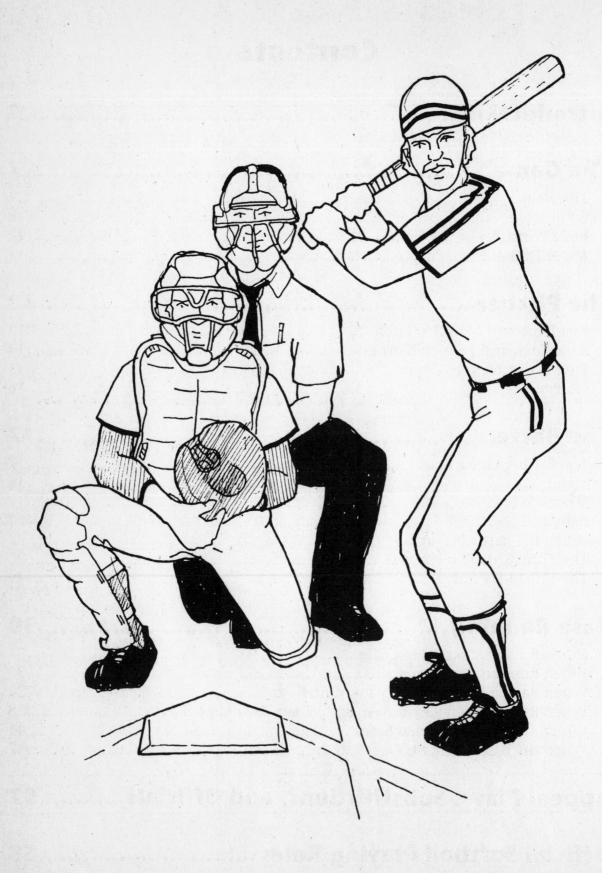

Introduction

This book is intended as an introduction to the basic rules of softball. Its illustrated format and simple language offer an entertaining and enjoyable way to learn the rules of the two main variants of the game, fast pitch and slow pitch. The official rules are sometimes technical and complicated, which makes it all the more important that both managers *and* players have a thorough knowledge of them. We hope that *Softball Rules in Pictures* will help novices learn the game's rules and also serve as a handy pre-season refresher course for veterans of the game.

The Amateur Softball Association of America (ASA) is the governing body of softball in the United States. Its codes and rules are generally accepted as the standard for two main types of softball, slow pitch and fast pitch, and their various spinoffs. The governing bodies of scholastic sports, the NCAA for example, or the NAIA and State High School Athletic Associations, have all slightly modified the ASA rules to suit their own needs but not in any way that drastically alters the character of the game.

The ASA provides more than a book of playing rules. It also organizes regional, state, and metro associations that sponsor tournaments and participate in national tournaments. The strict requirements and procedures of these tournaments (from the ban on drug use, the number of players on the roster, to the form that letters of protest may take) have all been codified by the ASA.

Competitors in these events may include all ages and abilities, from girls-under-12 fast pitch, to men's major industrial leagues, "masters" tournaments, and slow pitch. The ASA also supervises nonchampionship play; that is, the local softball that many of us play for recreation.

The association also evaluates the safety and legality of new equipment, supervises the training and certification of officials, and they even have a Hall of Fame.

A complete set of slow pitch, fast pitch, modified, and 16-inch rules can be found in the *Official Guide* published by the Amateur Softball Association of America, 2801 NE 50th Street, Oklahoma City, OK 73111.

OUTFIELD

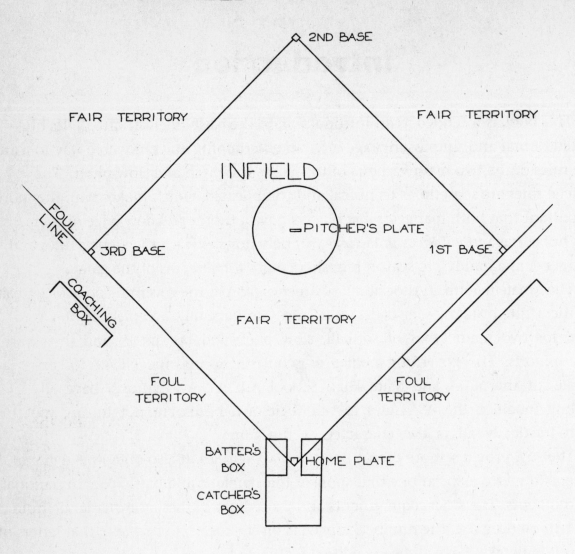

2ND BASE

FAIR TERRITORY   FAIR TERRITORY

INFIELD

FOUL LINE

PITCHER'S PLATE

3RD BASE   1ST BASE

COACHING BOX

FAIR TERRITORY

FOUL TERRITORY   FOUL TERRITORY

BATTER'S BOX   HOME PLATE

CATCHER'S BOX

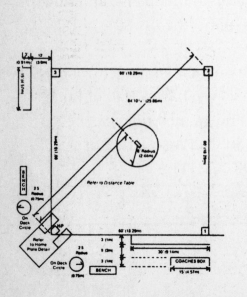

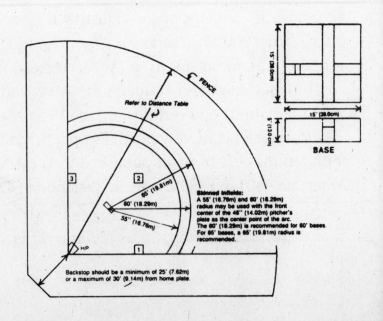

BASE

Skinned infields:
A 55' (16.76m) and 60' (18.29m) radius may be used with the front center of the 46'' (14.02m) pitcher's plate as the center point of the arc. The 60' (18.29m) is recommended for 60' bases. For 65' bases, a 65' (19.81m) radius is recommended.

Backstop should be a minimum of 25' (7.62m) or a maximum of 30' (9.14m) from home plate.

Chapter 1
The Game

The Field

Softball is played on a diamond-shaped field with bases located at each corner of the diamond. The field is divided into an infield (the area near or within the diamond, which is normally covered by the infielders) and an outfield (the area beyond the diamond, which is normally covered by the outfielders).

The dimensions of the field vary with the type of softball being played and the age and gender of the players. These variations ensure that the field is appropriate for the average strength and skill level of the players using it at the time. For example, in a ten-year-old boys' game the pitcher stands 35 feet from the batter, and in order to hit an out-of-the-park homer, the batter must swat the ball over an outfield fence 175 feet away. In a men's slow pitch, on the other hand, the pitcher throws from a full 65 feet away and the outfield fence is 300 feet away. Most field dimensions, including distance from pitching rubber to home plate, length between the bases, and distance to the outfield fence, will be slightly smaller for a fast pitch game than for a game of slow pitch.

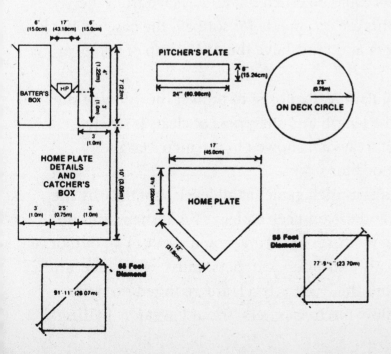

DISTANCE TABLE				
ADULT				
GAME	DIVISION	BASES	PITCHING	FENCES
Fast Pitch	Women	60' (18.29 m)	40' (12.19 m)	200' (60.96 m)
	Men	60' (18.29 m)	46' (14.02 m)	250' (76.20 m)
	Jr. Men	60' (18.29 m)	46' (14.02 m)	250' (76.20 m)
Modified	Women	60' (18.29 m)	40' (12.19 m)	200' (60.96 m)
	Men	60' (18.29 m)	46' (14.02 m)	265' (80.80 m)
Slow Pitch	Women	65' (19.81 m)	50' (15.24 m)	250' (76.20 m)
	Men	65' (19.81 m)	50' (15.24 m)	275' (83.82 m)
	Co-Ed	65' (19.81 m)	50' (15.24 m)	275' (83.82 m)
	Super	65' (19.81 m)	50' (15.24 m)	300' (91.44 m)
16 Inch Slow Pitch	Women	55' (16.76 m)	38' (11.58 m)	200' (60.96 m)
	Women	55' (16.76 m)	38' (11.58 m)	250' (76.20 m)

YOUTH					
GAME	DIVISION	BASES	PITCHING	FENCES	
				Minimum	Maximum
Slow Pitch	Girls 10-under	55' (16.76 m)	35' (10.67 m)	150' (45.72 m)	175' (53.34 m)
	Boys 10-under	55' (16.76 m)	35' (10.67 m)	150' (45.72 m)	175' (53.34 m)
	Girls 12-under	60' (18.29 m)	40' (12.19 m)	175' (53.34 m)	200' (60.96 m)
	Boys 12-under	60' (18.29 m)	40' (12.19 m)	175' (53.34 m)	200' (60.96 m)
	Girls 14-under	65' (19.81 m)	46' (14.02 m)	225' (68.58 m)	250' (76.20 m)
	Boys 14-under	65' (19.81 m)	46' (14.02 m)	250' (76.20 m)	275' (83.82 m)
	Girls 16-under	65' (19.81 m)	46' (14.02 m)	225' (68.58 m)	250' (76.20 m)
	Boys 16-under	65' (19.81 m)	46' (14.02 m)	275' (83.82 m)	300' (91.44 m)
	Girls 18-under	65' (19.81 m)	46' (14.02 m)	225' (68.58 m)	250' (76.20 m)
	Boys 18-under	65' (19.81 m)	50' (15.24 m)	275' (83.82 m)	300' (91.44 m)
Fast Pitch	Girls 10-under	55' (16.76 m)	35' (10.67 m)	150' (45.72 m)	175' (53.34 m)
	Boys 10-under	55' (16.76 m)	35' (10.67 m)	150' (45.72 m)	175' (53.34 m)
	Girls 12-under	60' (18.29 m)	35' (12.19 m)	175' (53.34 m)	200' (60.96 m)
	Boys 12-under	60' (18.29 m)	40' (12.19 m)	175' (53.34 m)	200' (60.96 m)
	Girls 14-under	60' (18.29 m)	40' (12.19 m)	175' (53.34 m)	200' (60.96 m)
	Boys 14-under	60' (18.29 m)	46' (12.19 m)	175' (53.34 m)	200' (60.96 m)
	Girls 16-under	60' (18.29 m)	40' (12.19 m)	200' (60.96 m)	225' (68.58 m)
	Boys 16-under	60' (18.29 m)	46' (12.19 m)	200' (60.96 m)	225' (68.58 m)
	Girls 18-under	60' (18.29 m)	40' (12.19 m)	200' (60.96 m)	225' (68.58 m)
	Boys 18-under	60' (18.29 m)	46' (12.19 m)	200' (60.96 m)	225' (68.58 m)

Equipment

Regulations also govern the size, weight, and shape of bats, balls, gloves, bases, and virtually all equipment used in the game. For example, teams are required to have uniforms, and the uniforms should be identical down to the caps and undershirts.

It is particularly important that players use only officially approved equipment. A batter can be called out for using an illegal bat and ejected for using an altered bat. Only the catcher and the first baseman are allowed to use first baseman's mitts. Other players seen using mitts could be called out and ejected from the game. While baseball gloves and mitts are acceptable for softball, the baseball bat is not. An official softball bat is thinner and must have the ASA stamp of approval prominently displayed.

Softball has some equipment regulations that exist to protect the safety of the players. Shoes must be worn, and the length and sharpness of cleats is strictly controlled. Although metal baseball spikes are allowed in the men's leagues, molded rubber cleats are recommended for safety.

Batting helmets must be worn in fast-pitch games at all levels, not only by the batter but also by the base runners and the on-deck batter as he or she warms up. Refusal to wear them while running the bases or batting could result in an out, or even ejection from the game. All fast-pitch catchers must wear face and throat protectors, and catchers on the youth level are required to wear full protection. Youth league slow-pitch catchers should wear a batting helmet.

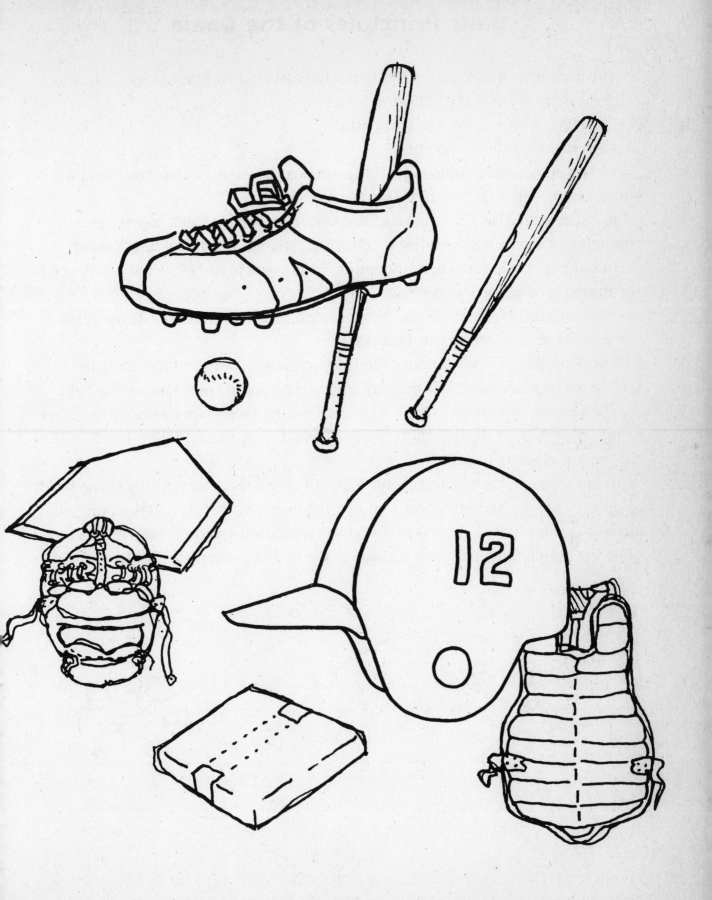

Basic Principles of the Game

The basic play of softball is very similar to baseball. Fast pitch, slow pitch, and other versions all share the following basics:

The object of the game is to score runs.

Each run counts as one point.

Batters become base runners and base runners are moved around the diamond when a batter hits a fair ball or is awarded a base.

Runs are scored each time a batter becomes a base runner and, moving in a counterclockwise direction, safely touches first, second, third, and home plates.

In order to score, the base runner must reach home plate before the third out of the inning is called against his team.

The "offensive" team is the team at bat. The "defensive" team plays the field, trying to stop the base runners.

The defenders may be stationed almost anywhere in fair territory. Only the pitcher and catcher must start the play from their assigned positions on the field.

The game is divided into innings. In each inning each team has one turn-at-bat (offense). While at bat, each team is allowed three outs. After three outs, the teams change places.

There are seven innings in a regulation softball game. However, there is no need to play the second half of the last inning if the team that bats last in the inning is already winning. If the game is tied after the regulation seven innings, extra innings are played until one team is ahead at the end of a complete inning.

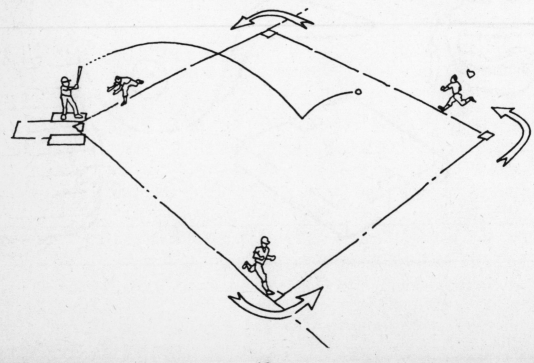

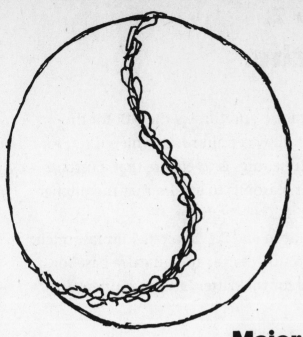
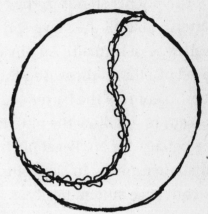

Major Differences

Along with these and other shared elements, the various forms of softball have some basic differences. Each type has a number of rules that regulate the style and speed of pitching.

For example, *modified pitch* eliminates two of the fastest and most difficult-to-hit pitches (the "windmill" and the "slingshot") that are used in straight fast-pitch softball. Slow-pitch rules require, among other things, that the ball travel within minimum and maximum limits of arc when pitched. One form of slow pitch is played with a ball that is 16 inches in diameter, which is much larger than the standard 12-inch ball.

Since the ball is easier to hit in slow pitch, the field dimensions are larger. It's not just that the outfield fence is farther away but the distance between pitching rubber and home plate is longer, which in turn makes the base paths longer.

Since slow pitch has a larger field, it uses more players than fast pitch. Fast pitch is played with nine (like baseball), slow pitch with ten, adding an extra player to the outfield. Of course, even more players may participate as substitutes or "designated players" (more on this later). Only 10 or 12 players may be used in a co-ed game so that the gender balance can be maintained. If 12 players are being used, one of the extra players must be male, the other female.

Slow pitch, unlike baseball or fast pitch, sets limits on the number of out-of-the-park home runs allowed per inning. Depending on the league's classification, this number can range from zero to 12. The batter will be called out for any home runs hit in excess of the limit.

Chapter 2
The Pitcher

The pitcher stands in the center of the diamond and throws the ball for the batters. Like all the players, the pitcher must follow certain rules, which differ for each type of softball. An obvious reason for these rules is to ensure that a certain speed of pitch is thrown to the batter. Another reason is to ensure that the pitcher doesn't confuse the batter and base runners with "fake" pitches.

Failure to follow the pitching rules will result in an "illegal pitch." In fast pitch, the penalty for an illegal pitch is a ball called for the batter and an extra base for any base runners. In slow pitch, a ball is called for the batter but the runners do not advance automatically.

Fast Pitch and Modified Pitch

Men's and women's fast pitch softball have rule variations that determine the stance of the pitcher, but both games require the pitcher and the catcher to be in position before the pitcher is considered ready to pitch. The catcher must stay inside the catcher's box until the ball has left the pitcher's hand. When stepping up to the pitcher's plate, the pitcher should approach with both hands separated. The ball may be held in either the glove or the throwing hand. For men, one foot must be placed on the pitching plate; the other may be on or behind the plate. Women must have both feet on the pitching plate. In either case the shoulders should be squarely facing the batter. Only at this time may the pitcher receive brief signals from the catcher.

When the pitcher is ready, both hands must be brought together holding the ball still in front of the body, for from one to ten seconds. The moment the pitcher takes one hand off the ball, the pitch proper has begun.

The pitcher may use any windup, but it is illegal to reverse the forward motion of the windup before the pitch is released. This will prevent the pitcher from throwing "fakes."

In men's play, the ball must be thrown with an underhanded motion with the hand below the hip. The wrist may not be further from the body than the elbow. When the pitcher takes a step forward, it must be taken at the same time as the delivery of the ball. The pitcher's other foot must remain on the pitching rubber until the forward stepping foot has touched the ground.

As mentioned earlier, women start with a different ready-to-pitch stance, and so the pitcher may allow her pivot foot to drag forward, off the pitching plate, before her other foot touches the ground. She must make sure that her pivot foot, in leaving the pitching plate, remains in contact with the ground.

Unless there are base runners that may be stealing the next base, the catcher should return the ball only to the pitcher. This eliminates wasting time and the danger that a ball could actually be called for this infraction.

The pitching in modified pitch softball is very similar to fast pitch, but the ball is slowed down a bit, since all pitchers (not just women) begin with both feet on the pitching plate. In modified ball, the pitcher may not use the windmill or sling-shot pitches, which feature a side arm delivery.

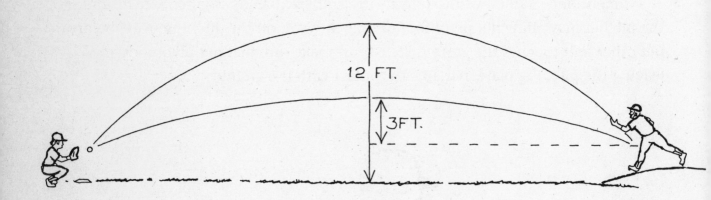

Slow Pitch and 16-inch Slow Pitch

Slow pitching regulations are a simplified version of the fast pitch regulations. To start, a pitcher must simply pause with the ball held in front of his or her body, keeping a foot on the pitching plate. When pitching, the pivot foot must be kept in contact with the rubber but the other foot may step forward, or even backward during the pitch. In slow pitch softball the ball must not be delivered at excessive speed (in the judgment of the umpire) and two such offenses could result in the removal of the pitcher from the pitching position (he or she can still play another defensive position). After leaving the pitcher's hand, the ball must arc at least six feet from the ground before crossing home plate. A pitch's maximum height off the ground in slow pitch is 12 feet. The catcher, except in trying to throw out a runner after a fly ball, should always return the ball directly to the pitcher.

Pitching Infractions

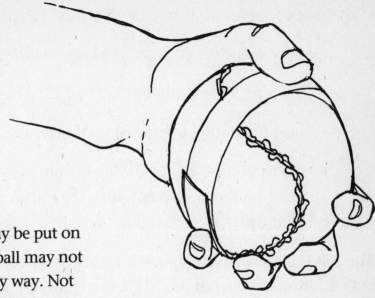

No "foreign substance" may be put on the hand or the ball, and the ball may not be intentionally defaced in any way. Not only will an illegal pitch be called, but the pitcher could be ejected from the game.

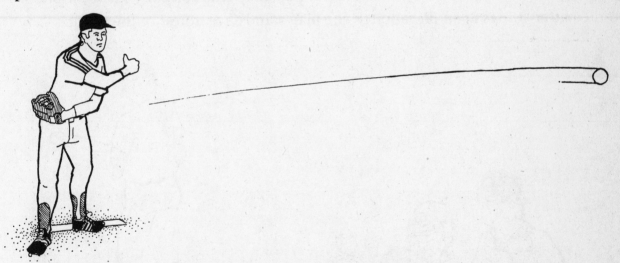

A pitch will be ruled illegal if the pitcher, after taking the pitching position, throws to a base while a foot is still in contact with the pitcher's plate. If the pitcher wants to throw to a base, he must first step back off the pitching plate. This eliminates "foot fakes" by the pitcher.

The pitcher may not take the pitching position unless he has the ball.

A pitch may not be rolled or bounced on the ground.

A fast-pitch pitcher may complete only one revolution when using the windmill delivery.

A pitcher may have only one conference per inning with a manager or team mate from the dugout.

No Pitch

A no-pitch call by the umpire cancels any action resulting from a pitch. Some plays that result in a no pitch are:

- pitching before a base runner has had time to return to base;

- pitching if the batter has not had time to get ready;

- pitching during a suspension of play; and

- the ball slipping loose during the pitchers wind up. (A ball will be called, and in fast pitch the runners may advance at their own risk.)

The ball is dead when a no pitch is called. The base runners may not advance or be put out. However, in fast pitch, if a batter hits an illegal pitch and reaches first safely and all the base runners advance at least one base, the play will be allowed to stand. (This is what the runners would have been awarded anyway.) In slow pitch, if the batter swings at an illegal pitch the play stands, regardless of the result.

Chapter 3
The Batter

The Batting Order

A written batting order must be given to the umpire before the game and must be followed throughout the game. If an error in the batting order is discovered and properly appealed before the batter completes his turn at bat, the error is corrected and all play, including balls and strikes, stands. If the team in the field discovers the error after the incorrect batter completes his turn at bat but before the first pitch to the next batter, it may appeal to the umpire who will call out the batter who should have been up and will return any runners who advanced while the incorrect player was at bat. If the error is discovered later in the game, all play stands.

Co-ed games always alternate male and female players in the batting order. They also require gender balance in the placing of the defensive players in the field.

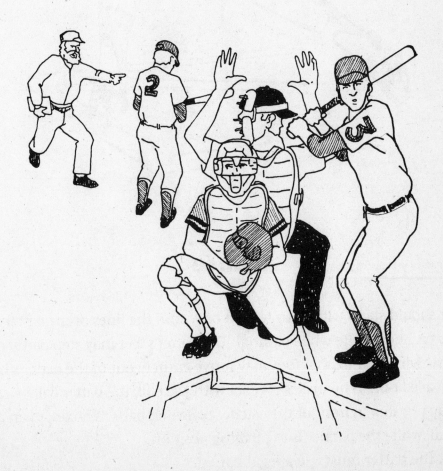

Stance

The batter should stand with both feet on or within the lines of the batter's box, and must not step on home plate while batting. The batter's feet may step partly out of the box during the swing, but neither foot may move entirely out of the batter's box, or the batter will be called out. If he makes contact with the ball, the batter will be called out. The batter may not step in front of the catcher or switch batter's boxes, in an attempt to disrupt a signal, while the pitcher is in pitching position.

Of course, the batter must use a legal bat.

Strikes

As we all know, three strikes and "yer out!" You must go back to the dugout and wait for a chance to redeem yourself later. A strike will be called when:

- the batter swings at a pitched ball and misses it (even if the ball hits the batter);

- a pitched ball enters the strike zone over home plate and the batter does not swing at it (again, even if it hits the batter).

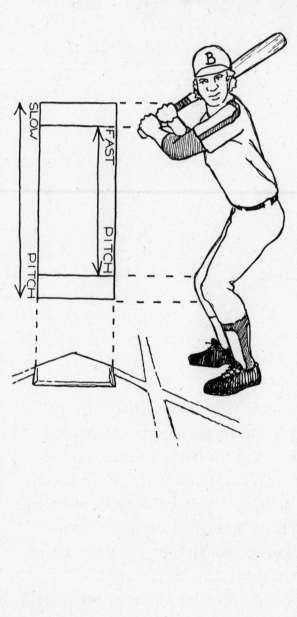

In fast pitch, a strike is called when the ball is hit into foul territory and is not caught on the fly—except if the batter already has two strikes. In that case, the "count" remains at two strikes.

In slow pitch, however, foul balls will be counted even for the third strike. This prevents batters fouling off balls all afternoon waiting for the perfect pitch.

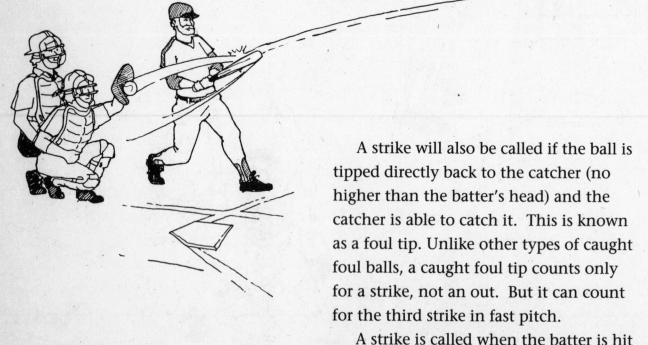

A strike will also be called if the ball is tipped directly back to the catcher (no higher than the batter's head) and the catcher is able to catch it. This is known as a foul tip. Unlike other types of caught foul balls, a caught foul tip counts only for a strike, not an out. But it can count for the third strike in fast pitch.

A strike is called when the batter is hit with his own batted ball while still in the batter's box—but will not count for the third strike.

Balls

If, during his turn at bat, the pitcher has four balls called against him or her, the batter becomes a base runner and will "walk" to first base without danger of being put out.

Some of the reasons a ball will be called are the following:

The pitch is not in the strike zone, so the batter doesn't swing at it. This includes pitches that hit home plate or even land before they get there.

A ball is illegally pitched. In slow pitch, since the batter has time to hear the call and check his or her swing, a ball will be called only if the batter does not swing at the pitch.

In slow pitch, a ball will be called if the batter is hit on any part of the body, outside the strike zone, by a pitch at which he did not swing. In fast pitch, this is a more serious offense; the batter could have been injured, and therefore is awarded a base.

The status of the ball during play is one of the most important differences between fast pitch and slow pitch and this has a great effect on the player' actions. In fast pitch, the ball remains live after a ball or strike is called and the runners can advance. In slow pitch, the ball is dead and the runners must tag back where they were and wait for the next pitch.

When the Batter Is Out

Here are some common situations in which the batter will be called out. If he or she:

- has three strikes called, even if the ball hits the batter or is a foul tip;

- hits a fly ball fair or foul, which is caught by an opponent;

- in fast pitch, bunts or chops the ball foul with two strikes already called;

- in slow pitch, bunts or chops the ball, regardless of what other circumstances exist;

"Yer out!"

- doesn't step into the batter's box promptly—ten seconds after the umpire has called for the batter;

- steps into the batter's box with an illegal or altered bat;

- steps from one batter's box to the other when the pitcher is ready to pitch;

- plants a foot all the way out of the batter's box onto home plate and swings and makes contact with the ball.

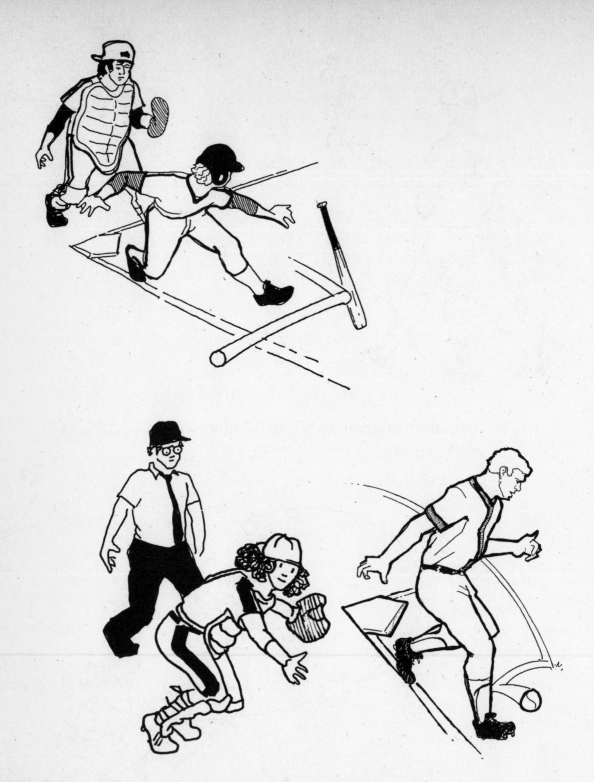

The batter will be out if he intentionally hits the ball twice. If he unintention-ally hits the ball twice, let's say when dropping the bat and running to first base, he will still be called out if the double hit effects the play in his favor.

Batters are out if, after leaving the batter's box, they are hit by a fair-hit ball before the ball has been played by a fielder.

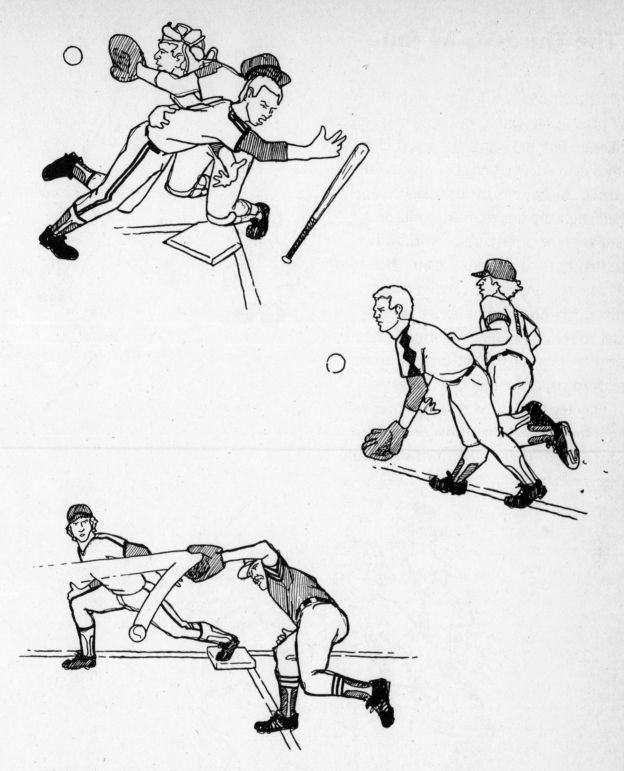

If there are two outs, a batter who interferes with a play at home plate is out. If there are less than two outs, the runner closest to home plate is out.

The batter is out if a preceding base runner intentionally interferes with or fails to give the right of way to a fielder trying to field a batted ball. In an obvious double play situation, the runner is also out.

The batter is out if, in the judgment of the umpire, a fielder intentionally drops a fly ball in order to create a force play when a runner is on first base.

The Third-Strike Rule

The third-strike rule represents the one time in fast pitch softball when three strikes do *not* make an out. This rule comes into effect when the catcher fails to catch the batter's third strike, except when there are less than two outs and first base is occupied. The less-than-two and first-base conditions are attached to this rule to prevent the catcher from deliberately dropping third strikes in order to set up double play situations. In all other situations, if the catcher drops the third strike the batter is not yet out but may try for first base. The batter is safe if he can beat the throw or avoid being tagged. There is no third-strike rule in slow pitch.

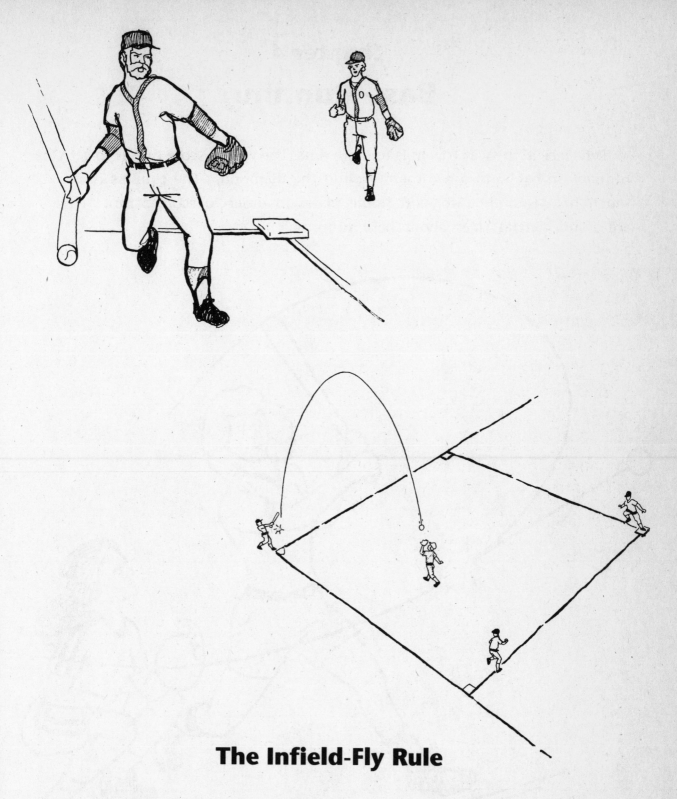

The Infield-Fly Rule

An infield fly is a fair fly ball that might be caught with ordinary effort by an infielder. The batter is out if he hits an infield fly, there are less than two outs, and runners are on first and second OR first, second, and third. Line drives and bunts are not infield flies. This rule was designed to remove the force play on the runner at first and prevent the intentional dropping of easily caught fly balls to create double play opportunities.

Chapter 4
Base Running

Let's face it, the way to win is to score runs. The way to score runs is to get your runners on base and move them around the diamond. The runners must touch first, second, third, and home plates in order to score a run. Here are some general rules about base running:

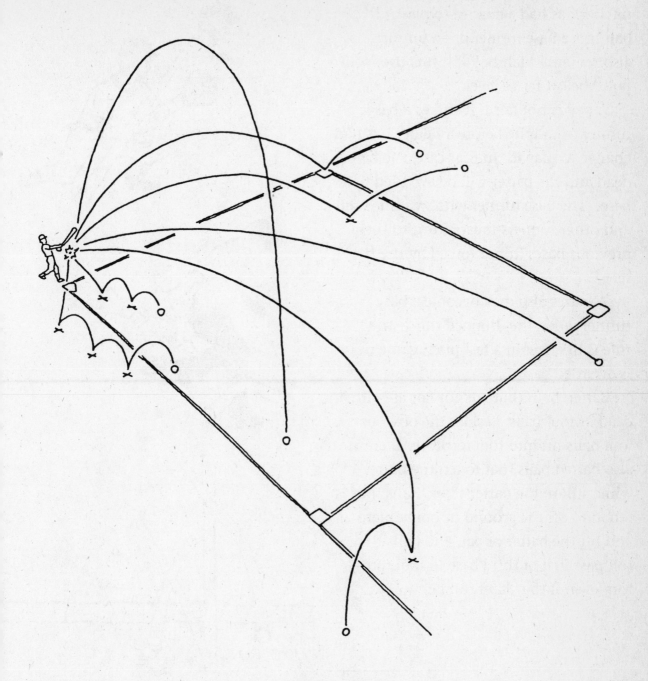

Fair Ball

The batter becomes a base runner when he or she hits a fair ball, is awarded a base, or when the third-strike rule comes into effect.

A fair ball is a legally batted ball that settles in fair territory (between the first- and third-base lines), even if it hits a base and then bounces foul.

It remains a fair ball and is in play even if, after a fielder other than the pitcher has had a chance to play it, the ball hits a base runner or an umpire. It also remains a fair ball if it hits the "foul pole" below fence level.

A ball is not fair if it strikes a base runner or umpire before a fielder has had chance to play it. In that case, the ball is dead and the batter will be awarded first base. The base runner who was hit is out and other runners must return to their previous bases (if not forced by the batter).

A batter also may become a base runner when the dropped third-strike rule is in effect in a fast pitch game or he is awarded bases.

Batted balls that are not fair are either dead or foul balls. Besides the obvious foul balls hit into foul territory, there are also batted balls that touch the batter while still in the batter's box, balls that rebound off the ground or home plate and hit the batter or bat, and balls that roll past first or third base in foul territory even if they later roll fair.

HOME RUN

HOME RUN

FAIR BALL

FOUL POLE

FAIR BALL

When Runners Are Forced

A base runner establishes the "right" to a base by touching it before being put out. He may hold the base until he has touched the next base.

When the batter becomes a base runner he might force other runners to move on. For example, when a player at bat becomes a base runner, the runner at first base is forced to move on to second base. When the batter becomes a base runner and the runner at first is forced, then a runner at second would also be forced to move to third, and if a runner also was on third, that runner would be forced to move on and try to tag home.

Base runners are not forced unless there are forced runners immediately behind them.

When Base Runners May Try for More Bases

Base runners may try for more bases when a fair ball is hit. And they may try for more bases after a legally caught fly ball, fair or foul, is first touched, but they must first tag the base they were at before they may run.

Base runners may try for more bases when the ball is overthrown, including a wild pitch in fast pitch, but not if thrown out of the park or into dead ball territory. If the latter occurs, they will be awarded bases. Of course, base runners must try for the next base when forced to do so by the batter or another runner who is forced.

An overthrown ball—the base runner is free to run.

When Runners May Leave Base and When They Must Return

As mentioned earlier one of the biggest differences between fast- and slow-pitch softball are the rules governing when a runner may leave base.

In slow pitch, a runner may legally leave base when a pitched ball reaches home plate. The ball is dead, however, on every not hit ball. Unlike fast pitch, the runners can't move to the next base unless the ball is batted. In fast pitch, a base runner may legally leave the base when a pitched ball leaves the pitcher's hand and may try for the next base whether a ball or strike is called or the ball is hit.

This lead-off is legal in fast pitch. Is it legal in slow pitch?

Base stealing is not allowed in slow pitch softball. A runner must return to base any time a pitched ball is not hit. All base runners, slow pitch or fast, must return to the base they occupy between pitches. A runner who has begun to advance cannot be stopped by a quick return of the ball to the pitcher, who simply gets ready for the next pitch, with ball in hand. The runner, however, must move on to the next base, or back to the one he or she was holding. When a foul ball is hit and the ball lands it is dead and the base runners must go back to the base occupied without danger of being put out.

The runner continues to second base.

The batter has been hit by the pitcher. The base runner must return to third.

Here are some other times a base runner must return to base:

- when a batter or base runner is called out for interference with the ball or a fielder;

- when the batter is hit by a pitched ball, whether a strike or a ball, but not if the runner is going to be advanced by the batter being awarded a base;

- when an infield fly is called and caught. If the fielder drops an infield fly the base runner may try to advance just as he would on any other dropped fly ball;

- when a ball is illegally batted; and

- if a batted ball hits the umpire before a defensive player other than the pitcher has had a chance to play it.

A base runner need not return to base if he or she is about to be awarded the next base.

When a Batter Is Awarded Bases

The batter is awarded first base or walked without danger of being put out when four balls are called. In slow pitch, the pitcher may simply inform the umpire that he or she intends to walk the batter. In fast pitch, the pitcher must actually throw four balls.

The batter will be awarded first base when a catcher (or any other fielder) obstructs or hinders him from hitting the ball.

In fast pitch, if a pitched ball outside the strike zone hits a batter, and the batter did not swing at it, then the batter is given first base.

The batter may be awarded more than one base in some cases: three, if a detached glove hits a batted ball; and, if this detached glove knocks down a ball that would have been a home run, the batter is awarded four bases (a home run).

There are several instances where base runners are awarded bases without risk.

All base runners are given the right to advance to the next base, or even beyond when forced to do so by the batter. Usually, this means base runners advance one base, if forced by a batter who is walked. But if the batter were awarded three bases, placing him or her on third base, then every base runner ahead of the batter would advance around the base path to home and score a run.

A base runner may move up one base without danger of being called out when a legally caught ball is carried unintentionally into dead ball territory. For example, if the player making the catch falls over a low outfield fence or into the dugout, runners may move to the next base. Balls intentionally carried into dead ball territory will result in a two base award.

A base runner is given the right to advance at least one base without risk when a fielder who is not playing the ball obstructs or impedes with a base runner. (This includes a fake tag when the fielder does not really have the ball.) In this case, the runners will all be awarded the bases they would have reached, according to the judgment of the umpire, had this infraction not happened.

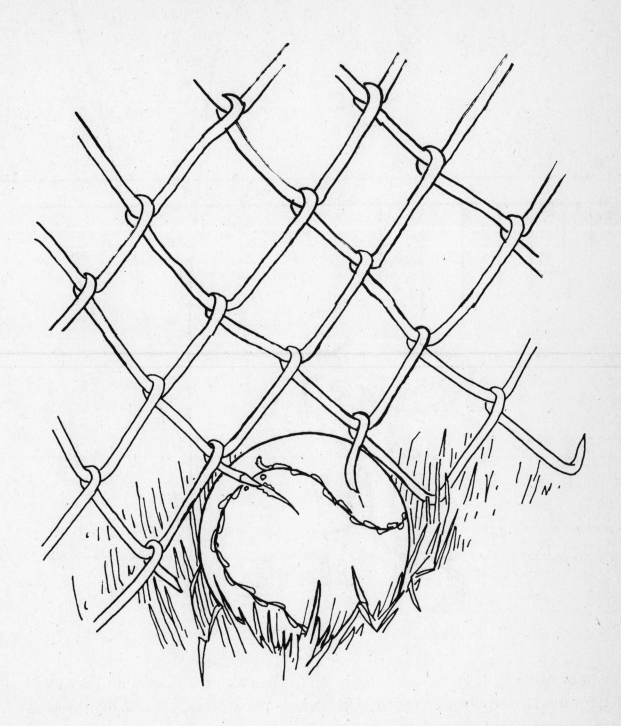

In fast pitch, base runners get a base when the pitch jams in the backstop. Since the ball is live, we don't want them coming all the way in while the catcher frantically tries to pry the ball loose. The runner also gets to move up one base if the pitcher is called for illegal pitch (the batter is awarded a ball).

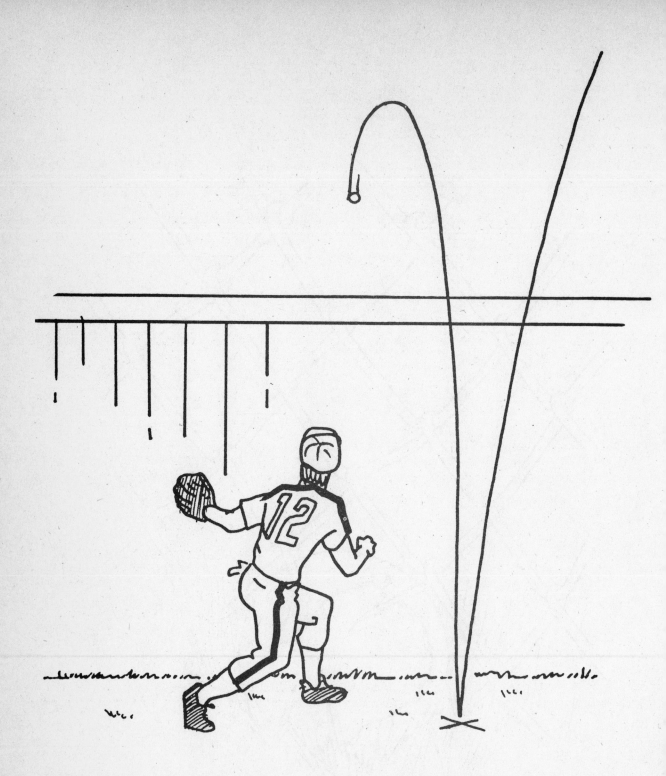

Runners will be awarded two bases if a fair ball rolls or bounces into dead ball territory. This is generally known as a "ground rule double." If a fielder throws a ball into dead ball territory, into the stands for example, base runners may advance two bases from where they were at the time of the throw.

Base runners are given the right to advance home without jeopardy when a fair fly ball hits the foul pole above fence height or flies into dead ball territory over the outfield fence. This is a very dry way of saying, "Home Run!"

When the Base Runner Is Out

Some common reasons a base runner will be called out:

- a fielder holding the ball touches the base to which the runner is forced before the runner does;

- a fielder tags the base runner with the ball when the runner is standing off the base, for example:
  — trying for the next base.
  — returning to base after a fair fly ball has been caught.
  — oversliding second or third base, or improperly overrunning first by moving toward second.

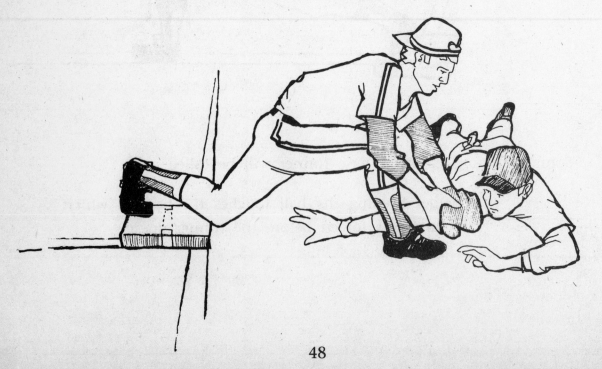

The base runner will be called out for leaving base early or for failing to return to base when the pitcher is preparing to pitch.

The runner is out if he or she runs outside the base path to avoid being tagged. However, the runner will not be called out for leaving the base path to yield the right of way to a defensive player fielding a batted ball.

A runner from third base will be out if the batter interferes with the play at the plate. If a base runner who has already been put out or has already scored interferes with the play at the base the next runner will be out.

The base runner will be called out for intentionally interfering with or failing to yield the right of way to a fielder playing the ball. If this interference is an obvious attempt to break up a double play, the runner immediately following will also be out.

If a runner is struck by a fair ball before it passes a fielder other than the pitcher, the runner is out.

If, while on the base path, a runner passes another runner who is not out, then the passing runner will be called out.

If two base runners occupy the same base at the same time and it is not a force play, the runner arriving last may be tagged out.

The batter/base runner will not be called out for overrunning first base, as long as he or she returns directly to the base.

A runner cannot be tagged out for failure to be in contact with a dislodged base, as long as the runner does not begin to try for the next base and tags in the approximate spot where the base should be.

If a judgment is made against a base runner on an appeal play, the runner is out.

Chapter 5
Appeal Plays, Substitutions, and Officials

Appeal Plays

An appeal play is made by the defensive team by claiming that a violation of certain rules has occurred. The appeal must be made by the defense before the next pitch is made to the batter. The ball may be in play during an appeal and ruling.

There are four major appeal plays: missing a base; leaving a base on a caught fly ball before it is first touched; batting out of order; and attempting to advance to second after a legal overrun of first base. Appeals are made during a live ball by touching the base missed or left too soon or by tagging the runner committing the violation (if the runner is still on the field). After the ball is dead, any infielder may make a verbal appeal to the umpire.

For example, a runner may be called out on appeal for missing home plate and then being tagged with the ball. But, if the runner does not realize the mistake and does not try to return and tag home, but moves toward the dugout instead, the catcher, holding the ball, may tag home plate.

The runner may be called out on appeal for missing a base, but the defender must tag the base or the runner. It is important to remember that if a runner misses a base, it does not affect the status or progress of any following runners (unless, of course, the runner's mistake results in his or her being called for the third out of the inning; then the inning is over). If a runner realizes his mistake and tries to return to the untagged base, the return must be made along the base paths. The runner cannot return if other runners have reached the missed base or if he or she has crossed home plate.

A runner may be tagged out for failing to return to first base immediately after overrunning or oversliding it. The runner may pivot left toward second base but may not make a move to advance, and must return immediately to first.

The defensive team may appeal if a batter bats out of turn. If this error is noticed by the batting team, the proper batter must take over the existing strike count and there is no penalty. However, if the defensive team notices and appeals, the batter who should have batted is out and any runners who may have advanced during that turn at bast must return to their previous positions.

If the error is not noticed until the incorrect batter has finished his turn at bat and the pitcher pitches even once to the next batter, then all play stands and nobody is out.

Substitutions

It's not always so easy to notice an error in the batting order. That's because substitutions may be made for any of the starting players during any dead ball situation. All batting and fielding substitutions must be reported to the plate umpire. New players must take the place of the players they replaced in the batting order.

To give the manager an even bigger clerical headache, the replaced player can come back into the game once; the next time he or she leaves, it's for the rest of the game. In addition, when the replaced player does return to bat it must be in the same place in the batting order.

But that's not the end of the rules for special substitutes. Fast pitch has a designated player or D.P. and slow pitch has an extra player, which is a simplified version of fast pitch's D.P. Each has its own set of rules.

The designated player bats for one of the nine fielders who then does not bat. The D.P. may also substitute for another player on defense and this player continues to bat. The D.P. may leave the game, and re-enter once, just like any other starting player.

Slow pitch's extra player is an eleventh player, listed on the batting order at the beginning of the game, and this extra player keeps the same position in the batting order all game. All eleven players must bat and any ten can play defense during a given inning.

Illegal substitutions (such as failure to report when entering or reentering) are not appeal plays. But it's very important for a manager to keep track of all substitutions and take advantage of any momentary mental lapse by opponents that brings a substitute to the plate in the wrong order.

Officials

Umpires are in complete charge and authority once they arrive on the field and can make decisions on situations not specifically covered in the rules. A manager may question an umpire's interpretation of the rules but will never successfully challenge an umpire's judgment. For example, only the umpire decides whether a ball is fair or foul. If there is one umpire, he should play behind the plate. When there are two umpires, a "plate" umpire and a "base" umpire, the plate umpire is the head umpire. Even so, both officials have equal authority to:

- call a runner out for leaving base early;
- call illegal pitches;
- eject players.

They may ask each other for help if the other umpire had a better angle to see the play.

It is important to remember that for appeal-type violations, umpires will not call a player out or even give any indication that they have seen an appeal-type violation. They will merely wait a brief time to see if an appeal is made.

It is the umpire's duty to stop the game if conditions become unsafe. The umpire may forfeit a game if a team is late, doesn't have enough players (teams can't play shorthanded) or is particularly unruly, for example, if an ejected player refuses to leave the field. An umpire may suspend play at any time. If he calls a game, let's say for darkness, after five innings, the score in the standings will count as if it had been a full game. The official scorers keep the written batting orders and the box score, including runs, hits, errors, runs batted in, and many other items.

Remember, the rules state that at no time may players make their opponents or the officials the butt of insults or disparaging remarks. Any player or team member may be ejected.

Even this simple outline of the basics demonstrates that officials—umpires, official scorers, and other league officials—have many responsibilities. Indeed, they have difficult jobs, but their main concern is to ensure that everyone on the field plays fairly and enjoys the game. Players should make every effort to work with these officials and help make their jobs easier.

SOFTBALL PLAYING RULES

Wherever "*he*" or "*him*" or their related pronouns may appear in this rule book either as words or as parts of words, they have been used for literary purposes and are meant in their generic sense (i.e., to include all humankind, or both male and female sexes).

The words "*Junior Olympic*" or the initials "*J.O.*" refer to youth softball.

New rules are highlighted in each section. All plays are italicized whether pertaining to new or old rules.
► *NOT ITALICIZED WITH THIS MARKING MEANS CHANGE IN WORDING FOR CLARIFICATION ONLY. NO CHANGE IS MADE IN THE RULE.*
Read the "Points of Emphasis" at the end of the rules to help clarify various selected rules.

RULE 1. DEFINITIONS

Sec. 1 ALTERED BAT. A bat is considered altered when the physical structure of a legal softball bat has been changed. Replacing the handle of a metal bat with a wooden or other type handle, inserting material inside the bat, applying excessive tape (more than two layers) to the bat grip, or painting a bat at the top or bottom for other than identification purposes are examples of altering a bat. Replacing the grip with another legal grip is not considered altering the bat. A "flare" or "cone" grip attached to the bat is considered an altered bat. (See Rule 7, Séc. 1d for penalty.)

PLAY —   B1 hits two-base hit with an aluminum bat containing a wooden handle. RULING — The ball is dead, batter-runner is out, and baserunners may not advance. The batter-runner is ejected for using an altered bat.

Sec. 2. APPEAL PLAY. An appeal play is a play on which an umpire may not make a decision until requested by a manager, coach, or player. The appeal must be made before the next legal or illegal pitch, or before the defensive team has left the field. The defensive team has "left the field" when the pitcher and all infielders have clearly vacated their normal fielding positions and have left fair territory on their way to the bench or dugout area.

PLAY —   With R1 on first, B2 hits a double. R1 goes to third but fails to touch second. Umpire observes this, but no appeal is made. B2 goes to second. Since no appeal was made, is the procedure the same as if R1 had touched second? RULING — Yes.

Sec. 3 BASE ON BALLS. A base on balls permits a batter to gain first base without liability to be put out and is awarded to a batter by the umpire when four pitches are judged to be balls. (SP ONLY) If the pitcher desires to walk a batter intentionally, he may do so by notifying the plate umpire who shall award the batter first base (Rule 8, Sec. 2c).

Sec. 4. BASE PATH. A base path is an imaginary line 3 feet (0.91 m) on either side of a direct line between the bases (Also refer to Rule 8, Section 8a).

Sec. 5. BASERUNNER. A baserunner is a player of the team at bat who has finished his turn at bat, reached first base, and has not yet been put out.

Sec. 6. BATTED BALL. A batted ball is any ball that hits the bat, or is hit by the bat, and lands either in fair or foul territory. No intention to hit the ball is necessary.

Sec. 7. BATTER'S BOX. The batter's box is the area to which the batter is restricted while in position with the intention of helping his team to obtain runs. The lines are considered as being within the batter's box. Prior to the pitch, he may touch the lines, but no part of his foot may be outside the lines.

Sec. 8. BATTER-RUNNER. A batter-runner is a player who has finished his turn at bat but has not yet been put out or touched first base.

Sec. 9. BATTING ORDER. The batting order is the official listing of offensive players in the order in which members of that team must come to bat. When the lineup card is submitted, it shall also include each player's position.

Sec. 10. BLOCKED BALL. A blocked ball is a batted or thrown ball that is touched, stopped, or handled by a person not engaged in the game, or which touches any object that is not part of the official equipment or official playing area.
EFFECT — If any illegal offensive equipment prevented the defense from making an out, the ball is dead, interference will be ruled, the player being played on shall be declared out, and each other runner must return to the last base touched at the time of the dead ball declaration. If no apparent play is obvious, a blocked ball is ruled, no one is called out, and each runner must return to the last base touched at the time of the dead ball declaration. See Rule 8, Sec. 5g (play 4) for enforcement.
PLAY —   A blocked ball is called when (a) it hits the coach, (b) it strikes a spectator. RULING — (a) No, (b) Yes.

Sec. 11. BUNT. A bunt is a legally tapped ball not swung at, but intentionally met with the bat and tapped slowly within the infield.

Sec. 12. CATCH. A catch is a legally caught ball which occurs when the fielder catches a batted, pitched, or thrown ball with his hand(s) or glove. If the ball is merely held in the fielder's arm(s) or prevented from dropping to the ground by some part of the fielder's body, equipment, or clothing, the catch is not completed until the ball is in the grasp of the fielder's hand(s) or glove. It is not a catch if a fielder, immediately after he contacts the ball, collides with another player, umpire, or a fence, or falls to the ground and drops the ball as a result of the collision or falling to the ground. In establishing a valid catch, the fielder shall hold the ball long enough to prove he has complete control of it or that his release of the ball is voluntary and intentional. If a player drops the ball after reaching into his glove to remove it, or while in the act of throwing it, it is a valid catch.
NOTE: A ball which strikes anything other than a defensive player while it is in flight is ruled the same as if it struck the ground.

PLAY (1) —   A legal catch occurs when a fielder holds the ball (a) in his hand(s), (b) under his arm(s), (c) in his cap, (d) in his glove. RULING — (a) Yes, (b) No, (c) No, (d) Yes.

PLAY (2) —   B1 hits line drive which, after passing F3, strikes the umpire while the ball is over fair ground. The ball ricochets and is fielded by F4 while still in flight. RULING — This is not a catch. B1 would have to be thrown out or tagged out.

PLAY (3) —   F3 and F4 both attempt to field a fly ball. Without touching the ground, the ball strikes F4 on the head and, while still in the air (hasn't touched the ground), is caught by F3. RULING — This is a legally caught fly ball.

PLAY (4) —   B1 hits fly to F8. F8 gets the ball in his hand(s) but drops it (a) when he falls to the ground and rolls over, or (b) when he collides with a fielder or a wall, or (c) when he starts to throw to the infield. RULING — In (a) and (b) it is not a catch. In (c) it is a legal catch if ball was held long enough for F8 to regain his balance but is then dropped in a motion associated with an intended throw.

Sec. 13. CATCHER'S BOX. The catcher's box is that area within which the catcher must remain until:
a. (FP ONLY) The pitch is released. The lines are to be considered within the catcher's box.
b. (SP ONLY) The pitched ball is batted, touches the ground or plate, or reaches the catcher's box. The lines are to be considered within the catcher's box, and all parts of the catcher's body and/or equipment must be within the catcher's box until the pitched ball is batted or reaches the catcher's box. The catcher is considered within the box unless he touches the ground outside the catcher's box.

EFFECT — Sec. 13b: An illegal pitch shall be called immediately, and the batter will be awarded a ball, provided he does not swing at the illegal pitch.

NOTE: For catcher's box dimensions, see Rule 2, Sec. 4d.

Sec. 14. CHARGED CONFERENCE. A charged conference takes place when:
a. (Defensive Conference) The defensive team requests a suspension of play for any reason, and a representative (not in the field) of the defensive team enters the playing field and gives the umpire cause to believe that he has delivered a message (by any means) to the pitcher.
b. (Offensive Conference) The offensive team requests a suspension of play to allow the manager or other team representatives to confer with the batter and/or baserunners. Refer to Rule 5, Sec. 8.

Sec. 15. CHOPPED BALL. (SP ONLY) A chopped hit ball is one at which the batter strikes downward with a chopping motion of the bat so that the ball bounces high into the air.

Sec. 16. COACH. A coach is a member of the team at bat who takes his place within one of the coaches' boxes on the field to direct the players of his team in running the bases. Two coaches are allowed. One coach may have in his possession in the coach's box a scorebook, pen or pencil, and an indicator, all of which shall be used for scorekeeping or record keeping purposes only. No communication equipment is allowed.

Sec. 17. DEAD BALL. The ball is not in play and is not considered in play again until the pitcher has it in his possession, is within 8 feet (2.44 m) of the pitcher's plate, and play ball has been declared by the umpire. A dead ball line is considered in play. Refer to Rule 1, Sec. 52.

Sec. 18. DEFENSIVE TEAM. The defensive team is the team in the field.

Sec. 19. DISLODGED BASE. A dislodged base is a base displaced from its proper position.

Sec. 20. DOUBLE PLAY. A double play is a play by the defense resulting in two offensive players being legally put out as a result of continuous action.

Sec. 21. FAIR BALL. A fair ball is a batted ball that:
a. Settles or is touched on or over fair territory between home and first base or between home and third base.
b. Bounds or rolls past first or third base on or over fair territory.
c. Bounds over any part of the first or third base bag, regardless of where the ball hits after going over the bag.
d. While on or over fair territory, touches the person, attached equipment, or clothing of a player or an umpire.
e. Touches first, second, or third base.
f. First falls or is first touched on or over fair territory beyond first, second, or third base.
g. While over fair territory, passes out of the playing field beyond the outfield fence.
h. Hits the foul pole above the fence level.

NOTE: A fair fly shall be judged according to the relative position of the ball and the foul line, including the foul pole, and not as to whether the fielder is on fair or foul territory at the time he touches the ball. It does not matter whether the ball first touches fair or foul territory, as long as it does not touch anything foreign to the natural ground in foul territory and complies with all other aspects of a fair ball.

PLAY (1) —   Batted ball settles on home plate. RULING — Fair ball.

PLAY (2) —   Batted ball first hits foul ground and, without touching any foreign object, rolls into fair territory between first and home or third and home where it settles. RULING — Fair ball.

PLAY (3) —   Batted ball rolls against bat in fair territory and (a) remains in fair territory or (b) rolls untouched into foul territory. RULING — A fair ball in (a) and a foul ball in (b).

Sec. 22. FAIR TERRITORY. Fair territory is that part of the playing field within, and including, the first and third base foul lines from home plate to the bottom of the extreme playing field fence and perpendicularly upward.

Sec. 23. FAKE TAG. A form of obstruction by a fielder who neither has the ball nor is about to receive the ball, and which impedes the progress of a runner either advancing or returning to a base. The runner does not have to stop or slide. Merely slowing down when a fake tag is administered would constitute obstruction. NOTE: Under Rule 8, Sec. 5b (3), a player may be removed from the game for a fake tag infraction.

Sec. 24. FIELDER. A fielder is any player of the team in the field.

Sec. 25. FLY BALL. A fly ball is any fair or foul ball batted into the air.

Sec. 26. FORCE OUT. A force out is an out which may be made only when a baserunner loses the right to the base he is occupying because the batter becomes a batter-runner, and before the batter-runner or a succeeding baserunner has been put out.

NOTE: If the forced runner, after touching the next base, retreats for any reason towards the base he had last occupied, the force play is reinstated, and he may again be put out if the defense tags the base to which he is forced.

PLAY (1) — *R1 is on first base. B2 hits sharp grounder to F3 who first touches first base and then touches R1 who is still on first base. RULING — Only B2 is out. F3's act eliminated the force, thereby permitting R1 to remain on first.*

PLAY (2) — *R1 on 1B when B2 hits a short fly ball to left field. R1 goes approximately 15 feet off base waiting to see if the ball will be caught. B2 rounds 1B and passes R1, and the umpire calls B2 out. The ball drops in for a base hit. R1 advances to 2B, and F4, with the ball, tags 2B before R1 slides into the base. RULING: The force out is removed when B2 passes R1; therefore, F4 had to tag R1. The runner is safe sliding into 2B if he was not tagged.*

Sec. 27. FOUL BALL. A foul ball is a batted ball that:
a. Settles or is touched on or over foul territory between home and first base or between home and third base.
b. Bounds or rolls past first or third base on or over foul territory.
c. While on or over foul territory, touches the person, attached equipment, or clothing of a player or an umpire, or any object foreign to the natural ground and provided a fair ball declaration had not been made prior to the ball entering foul territory..
d. First falls or is first touched on or over foul territory beyond first or third base.
e. Touches the batter or the bat a second time while the ball is within the batter's box.
f. Immediately rebounds up from the ground or home plate and hits the bat a second time while the batter is in the batter's box.

NOTE: A foul fly shall be judged according to the relative position of the ball and the foul line, including the foul pole, and not as to whether the fielder is on foul or fair territory at the time he touches the ball.

PLAY (1) — *A fair ball is called when (a) the ball hits the bag and deflects into foul territory, (b) the ball bounds from the infield over the base and lands in foul territory, (c) the ball lands within the confines of the infield and rolls foul without being touched by a fielder. RULING — (a) Correct, (b) Correct, (c) False.*

PLAY (2) — *Bat of B1 breaks into pieces as a result of hitting a pitch. The batted ball, bounding on foul territory in direction of third base, then hits the barrel of the bat, causing the ball to roll into fair territory in front of third base. F5 fields the ball and throws it to F3 who tags first base before B1 reaches it. RULING — Foul ball, but B1 is not out for hitting ball a second time.*

Sec. 28. FOUL TIP. A foul tip is a batted ball which goes directly from the bat, not higher than the batter's head, to the catcher's hand(s) and is legally caught by the catcher.

NOTE: It is not a foul tip unless caught, and any foul tip that is caught is a strike. In fast pitch and 16" slow pitch, the ball is in play. In slow pitch the ball is dead. It is not a catch if it is a rebound, unless the ball first touched the catcher's hand(s) or glove.

PLAY (1) — *Ball goes directly from bat and rebounds from protector (a) of F2 after having touched his glove, (b) of F2 without first having touched his glove, (c) of umpire after having first touched glove of F2, (d) of umpire without first having touched glove of F2. In each case the ball rebounds into glove of F2 and is held. RULING — In (a) it is a foul tip and a strike. In (b), (c), and (d) it is a foul, with ball becoming dead when it touched F2 in (b) or umpire in (c) and (d).*

PLAY (2) — *(FP ONLY) With R1 on second, B2 hits foul tip. May R1 advance without retouching second? Also, does it make any difference if the catcher drops the batted ball? RULING — A foul tip is the same as any strike; hence, R1 may advance without retouching. If batted ball is not caught, it is not a foul tip and is ruled a foul ball, in which case no runner may advance.*

Sec. 29. HELMET. a) A helmet worn by the batter, on-deck batter, or runner shall be the type which has safety features equal to or greater than those provided by the full plastic cap with padding on the inside. The liner-type helmet does not meet the rule specifications. b) JO slowpitch catchers must wear an approved batter's helmet with ear flaps, or the catcher's helmet and mask.

Sec. 30. HOME TEAM. The home team is the team on whose grounds the game is played. If the game is played on neutral ground, the home team shall be designated by mutual agreement or by a flip of a coin.

Sec. 31. ILLEGAL BAT. An illegal bat is one that does not meet the requirements of Rule 3, Sec. 1.

PLAY — *B1 hits a double to centerfield. Umpire notices bat has been tampered with, i.e., baseball bat honed down to softball size. RULING — Dead ball, and B1 is called out. Remove illegal piece of equipment from the game. This is an illegal bat.*

Sec. 32. ILLEGALLY BATTED BALL. An illegally batted ball occurs when:
a. A batter's entire foot is completely outside the lines of the batter's box and on the ground when he hits a ball fair or foul.
b. Any part of the batter's foot is touching home plate when he hits the ball fair or foul.
c. The batter hits the ball with an illegal bat.

PLAY (1) — *Batter hits a pitched ball while his entire foot is completely out of batter's box, in contact with the ground, and the ball goes directly into the stands behind home plate. RULING — Ball is dead. Batter is declared out.*

PLAY (2) — *F1 delivers ball to B1. B1 has one foot touching home plate as he swings and completely misses pitch. RULING — A strike is called. This is not an illegally batted ball. The ball must be hit (fair or foul) to enforce the illegally batted ball rule.*

Sec. 33. ILLEGALLY CAUGHT BALL. An illegally caught ball occurs when a fielder catches a batted or thrown ball with his cap, helmet, mask, protector, pocket, detached glove, or any part of his uniform that is detached from its proper place.

PLAY — *REFER TO RULE 1, Sec. 12.*

Sec. 34. ILLEGAL PITCHER. A player legally in the game, but one who may not pitch as a result of: (a) a pitcher who has been removed from the pitching position by the umpire as a result of two charged conferences in one inning, or (b) (SP ONLY) a pitcher who has been removed from the pitching position by the umpire as a result of pitching with excessive speed after a warning. PENALTY: If an illegal pitcher returns to the pitching position and has thrown one pitch, he is ejected from the game.

Sec. 35. ILLEGAL PLAYER. A player who has entered the game without reporting. When brought to the plate umpire's attention by the offended team after the first legal or illegal pitch, and before the team in violation informs the umpire, the use of an illegal player is removal of that player from the game and declared ineligible.

Sec. 36. INELIGIBLE PLAYER. A player who may no longer legally participate in the game because he has been removed by the umpire. An ineligible player may no longer participate as a player. The use of an ineligible player will constitute a forfeit.

Sec. 37. IN FLIGHT. *In flight* is the term used for any batted, thrown, or pitched ball which has not yet touched the ground or some object or person other than a fielder.

Sec. 38. IN JEOPARDY. *In jeopardy* is a term indicating that the ball is in play and an offensive player may be put out.

Sec. 39. INFIELD. The infield is that portion of the field in fair territory which includes areas normally covered by infielders.

Sec. 40. INFIELD FLY. An infield fly is a fair fly ball (not including a line drive or an attempted bunt) which can be caught by an infielder with ordinary effort when first and second bases or first, second, and third bases are occupied before two are out. The pitcher, catcher, and any outfielder who positions himself in the infield on the play shall be considered infielders for the purpose of this rule.
NOTE: When it seems apparent that a batted ball will be an infield fly, the umpire shall immediately declare, "INFIELD FLY. THE BATTER IS OUT," for the benefit of the runners. If the ball is near a foul line, the umpire shall declare, "INFIELD FLY. THE BATTER IS OUT IF FAIR."

The ball is alive, and runners may advance at the risk of the ball being caught or retouch and advance after the ball is touched, the same as on any fly ball. If the hit becomes a foul ball, it is treated the same as any foul.

If a declared infield fly is allowed to fall untouched to the ground and bounces foul before passing first or third base, it is a foul ball. If a declared infield fly falls untouched to the ground outside the foul lines and bounces fair before passing first or third base, it is an infield fly.

PLAY (1) — *R1 and R2 are on second and first bases respectively with none out. B3 hits a high pop foul between home and first base which F3 loses sight of in the sun. The infield fly is declared by the umpire(s). Ball lands on foul ground without being touched and rolls into fair territory halfway between home and first base. F1 picks up ball and throws to F4 covering first, who touches R2 with ball while runner R2 is off base. RULING — Infield fly. B3 and R2 are both out.*

PLAY (2) — *R1 and R2 are on second and first bases respectively with one out. B3 hits a high fly ball which, in the judgement of the umpire, may be handled by the second baseman with reasonable effort. The infield fly rule is declared by the umpire. The second baseman intentionally drops the fly ball. Seeing the ball dropped, R1 runs to third base but is thrown out. RULING — B3 is out on the infield fly. The ball remains alive. R1 is also out since the infield fly takes precedence over the "intentionally dropped fly ball."*

Sec. 41. INNING. An inning is that portion of a game within which the teams alternate on offense and defense, and in which there are three outs for each team. A new inning begins immediately after the final out of the previous inning.

Sec. 42. INTERFERENCE. Interference is the act of an offensive player or team member which impedes or confuses a defensive player attempting to execute a play.

Sec. 43. JUNIOR OLYMPIC PLAYER. Any player 18 years and under who has not reached the 19th birthday prior to September 1. NOTE: If one or more J.O. Player(s) play on an adult team, it is considered playing in an adult league and adult rules will be in effect.

Sec. 44. LEGAL TOUCH. A legal touch occurs when a baserunner or batter-runner who is not touching a base is touched by the ball while it is securely held in a fielder's hand(s). The ball is not considered as having been securely held if it is juggled or dropped by the fielder after having touched the runner, unless the runner deliberately knocks the ball from the hand(s) of the fielder. It is sufficient for the runner to be touched with the glove or hand(s) holding the ball.

PLAY (1) — *B1 hits ground ball to first baseman who gathers in the ball, runs over to the first baseline, tags the runner, then juggles, bobbles, and drops the ball. RULING — Illegal touch. Runner is safe.*

PLAY (2) — *The catcher has the ball in his glove when he tags runner with the glove. Ball does not come into contact with the runner. RULING — Touching with the glove or hand(s) holding the ball is the same as touching with the ball. The runner is out.*

PLAY (3) — *While lying on the ground with ball in right hand, the first baseman tags first base with left hand prior to batter-runner reaching first base. RULING — Batter-runner is out. Legal touch.*

Sec. 45. LEGALLY CAUGHT BALL. A legally caught ball occurs when a fielder catches a batted, pitched, or thrown ball, provided it is not caught in the fielder's cap, helmet, mask, protector, pocket, detached glove, or any part of his uniform that is detached from its proper place on his person. It must be caught and firmly held with a hand or hands. A player may not be contacting anything in a dead ball area at the time of the catch.

Sec. 46. LINE DRIVE. A line drive is a fly ball that is batted sharply and directly into the playing field.

Sec. 47. OBSTRUCTION. Obstruction is the act of:
a. A defensive player or team member which hinders or prevents a batter from striking or hitting a pitched ball.
b. A fielder, (1) not in possession of the ball, (2) not in the act of fielding a batted ball, or (3) not about to receive a thrown ball which impedes the progress of a baserunner or batter-runner who is legally running bases.

Sec. 48. OFFENSIVE TEAM. The offensive team is the team at bat.

Sec. 49. ON-DECK BATTER. The on-deck batter is the offensive player whose name follows the name of the batter in the batting order. He shall take a position within the lines of the on-deck circle nearest his bench. (Refer to Rule 7, Sec. 13.)

Sec. 50. OUTFIELD. The outfield is that portion of the field which is outside the diamond formed by the baselines, or the area not normally covered by an infielder, and within the foul lines beyond first and third bases and boundaries of the grounds.

Sec. 51. OVERSLIDE. An overslide is the act of an offensive player when, as a runner, he overslides a base he is attempting to reach. It is usually caused when his momentum causes him to lose contact with the base, which then causes him to be in jeopardy. The batter-runner may overslide first base without being in jeopardy.

PLAY — *A runner overslides first base (a) during advance from home plate or (b) on return to first base after attempt to advance to second base. In either case he is tagged with ball while off base. RULING — (a) Safe, (b) Out.*

Sec. 52. OVERTHROW. An overthrow occurs when a thrown ball from a fielder goes beyond the boundary lines of the playing field (dead ball territory) or becomes a BLOCKED BALL. (Rule 1, Sec. 10)

Sec. 53. PASSED BALL. (FP ONLY) A passed ball is a legally delivered ball that should have been held or controlled by the catcher with ordinary effort.

Sec. 54. PIVOT FOOT. (FP ONLY) The pivot foot is that foot which must remain in contact with the pitcher's plate. Pushing off with the pivot foot from a place other than the pitcher's plate is illegal.

(SP ONLY) The pivot foot is that foot which the pitcher must keep in constant contact with the pitcher's plate until the ball is released.

NOTE: (16'' Slow Pitch) After a hesitation, the pivot foot may be removed during a pickoff situation but must be replaced in contact with the pitcher's plate before the pitch is released.

Sec. 55. PLAY BALL. *Play ball* is the term used by the plate umpire to indicate that play shall begin or be resumed when the pitcher has the ball in his possession and is within 8 feet (2.44 m) of the pitcher's plate. All defensive players except the catcher, who must be in his box, must be anywhere on fair ground to put the ball into play.

NOTE: (FP ONLY) See Rule 6, Sec. 7 for penalty.

Sec. 56. QUICK RETURN PITCH. A quick return pitch is one made by the pitcher with the obvious attempt to catch the batter off balance. This would be before the batter takes his desired position in the batter's box or while he is still off balance as a result of the previous pitch.

Sec. 57. RUNNER. The term *runner* means ''batter-runner'' or ''baserunner.''

Sec. 58. SACRIFICE FLY. A sacrifice fly is scored when, with fewer than two outs, a) the batter scores a runner with a fly ball or line drive that is caught; or b) the batter scores a runner with a fly ball or line drive that is dropped by an outfielder (or an infielder running into the outfield), and, in the scorer's judgement, the runner could have scored after the catch had the fly ball or line drive been caught.

Sec. 59. STARTING PITCHER. The player listed as a pitcher on the lineup card or official scorebook.

Sec. 60. STEALING. (FP ONLY) Stealing is the act of a baserunner attempting to advance during a pitch to the batter.

Sec. 61. STRIKE ZONE. (FP ONLY) The strike zone is that space over any part of home plate between the batter's arm pits and the top of his knees when he assumes a natural batting stance.

(SP ONLY) The strike zone is that space over any part of home plate between the batter's back shoulder and his knees when he assumes a natural batting stance.

Sec. 62. TIME. *Time* is the term used by the umpire to order the suspension of play.

Sec. 63. TRIPLE PLAY. A triple play is a continuous action play by the defense on which three offensive players are put out.

Sec. 64. TURN AT BAT. A turn at bat begins when a player first enters the batter's box and continues until he is put out or becomes a batter-runner.

Sec. 65. WILD PITCH. (FP ONLY) A wild pitch is a legally delivered ball so high, so low, or so wide of the plate that the catcher cannot catch or stop and control it with ordinary effort.

RULE 2. THE PLAYING FIELD

(Refer to Drawing Showing Official Dimensions of Softball Diamond)

Sec. 1. THE PLAYING FIELD IS THE AREA WITHIN WHICH THE BALL MAY BE LEGALLY PLAYED AND FIELDED. The playing field shall have a clear and unobstructed area between the foul lines and within the radius of the prescribed fence distances from home plate.
(Refer to FENCE DISTANCE Chart).

ADULT DIVISIONS	DISTANCES	
	Minimum	Maximum
Fast Pitch		
Women .... 200 ft. (60.96 m)		
Men .... 225 ft. (68.58 m)		250 ft. (76.20 m)*
Junior Men .... 225 ft. (68.58 m)		250 ft. (76.20 m)

*In case of inclement weather, maximum fence distance may be waived.

Modified		
Women .... 200 ft. (60.96 m)		
Men .... 265 ft. (80.80 m)		
Slow Pitch		
Women .... 250 ft. (76.20 m)		
Men .... 275 ft. (83.82 m)		
Co-Ed .... 275 ft. (83.82 m)		
Super .... 300 ft. (91.44 m)		

*Beginning in 1991, Men's Major and Super Division fence distance shall be 300 feet in national championship tournament play only.

16'' Slow Pitch		
Women .... 200 ft. (60.96 m)		
Men .... 250 ft. (76.20 m)		

YOUTH DIVISIONS	DISTANCES	
	Minimum	Maximum
Fast Pitch		
Girls 10-Under .... 150 ft. (45.72 m)		175 ft. (53.34 m)
Boys 10-Under .... 150 ft. (45.72 m)		175 ft. (53.34 m)
Girls 12-Under .... 175 ft. (53.34 m)		200 ft. (60.96 m)
Boys 12-Under .... 175 ft. (53.34 m)		200 ft. (60.96 m)
Girls 14-Under .... 175 ft. (53.34 m)		200 ft. (60.96 m)
Boys 14-Under .... 175 ft. (53.34 m)		200 ft. (60.96 m)
Girls 16-Under .... 200 ft. (60.96 m)		225 ft. (68.58 m)
Boys 16-Under .... 200 ft. (60.96 m)		225 ft. (68.58 m)
Girls 18-Under .... 200 ft. (60.96 m)		225 ft. (68.58 m)
Boys 18-Under .... 200 ft. (60.96 m)		225 ft. (68.58 m)
Slow Pitch		
Girls 10-Under .... 150 ft. (45.72 m)		175 ft. (53.34 m)
Boys 10-Under .... 150 ft. (45.72 m)		175 ft. (53.34 m)
Girls 12-Under .... 175 ft. (53.34 m)		200 ft. (60.96 m)
Boys 12-Under .... 175 ft. (53.34 m)		200 ft. (60.96 m)
Girls 14-Under .... 225 ft. (68.58 m)		250 ft. (76.20 m)
Boys 14-Under .... 250 ft. (76.20 m)		275 ft. (83.82 m)
Girls 16-Under .... 225 ft. (68.58 m)		250 ft. (76.20 m)
Boys 16-Under .... 275 ft. (83.82 m)		300 ft. (91.44 m)
Girls 18-Under .... 225 ft. (68.58 m)		250 ft. (76.20 m)
Boys 18-Under .... 275 ft. (83.82 m)		300 ft. (91.44 m)

Sec. 2. GROUND OR SPECIAL RULES ESTABLISHING THE LIMITS OF THE PLAYING FIELD MAY BE AGREED UPON BY LEAGUES OR OPPOSING TEAMS WHENEVER BACKSTOPS, FENCES, STANDS, VEHICLES, SPECTATORS, OR OTHER OBSTRUCTIONS ARE WITHIN THE PRESCRIBED AREA. Any obstruction on fair ground less than the prescribed fence distances from home plate (as outlined in Sec. 1 of this rule) should be clearly marked for the umpire's information.

Sec. 3. THE OFFICIAL DIAMOND SHALL HAVE BASE LINES AS FOLLOWS:

ADULT DIVISIONS	DISTANCES	YOUTH DIVISIONS	DISTANCES
Fast Pitch		Fast Pitch	
Women	60 ft. (18.29 m)	Girls 10-Under	55 ft. (16.76 m)
Men	60 ft. (18.29 m)	Boys 10-Under	55 ft. (16.76 m)
Junior Men	60 ft. (18.29 m)	Girls 12-Under	60 ft. (18.29 m)
		Boys 12-Under	60 ft. (18.29 m)
Modified		Girls 14-Under	60 ft. (18.29 m)
Women	60 ft. (18.29 m)	Boys 14-Under	60 ft. (18.29 m)
Men	60 ft. (18.29 m)	Girls 16-Under	60 ft. (18.29 m)
		Boys 16-Under	60 ft. (18.29 m)
Slow Pitch		Girls 18-Under	60 ft. (18.29 m)
Women	65 ft. (19.81 m)	Boys 18-Under	60 ft. (18.29 m)
Men	65 ft. (19.81 m)		
Co-ed	65 ft. (19.81 m)	Slow Pitch	
Super	65 ft. (19.81 m)	Girls 10-Under	55 ft. (16.76 m)
		Boys 10-Under	55 ft. (16.76 m)
16'' Slow Pitch		Girls 12-Under	60 ft. (18.29 m)
Women	55 ft. (16.76 m)	Boys 12-Under	60 ft. (18.29 m)
Men	55 ft. (16.76 m)	Girls 14-Under	65 ft. (19.81 m)
		Boys 14-Under	65 ft. (19.81 m)
		Girls 16-Under	65 ft. (19.81 m)
		Boys 16-Under	65 ft. (19.81 m)
		Girls 18-Under	65 ft. (19.81 m)
		Boys 18-Under	65 ft. (19.81 m)

THE OFFICIAL DIAMOND SHALL HAVE PITCHING DISTANCES AS FOLLOWS:

ADULT DIVISIONS	DISTANCES	YOUTH DIVISIONS	DISTANCES
Fast Pitch		Fast Pitch	
Women	40 ft. (12.19 m)	Girls 10-Under	35 ft. (10.67 m)
Men	46 ft. (14.02 m)	Boys 10-Under	35 ft. (10.67 m)
Junior Men	46 ft. (14.02 m)	Girls 12-Under	35 ft. (10.67 m)
Modified		Boys 12-Under	40 ft. (12.19 m)
Women	40 ft. (12.19 m)	Girls 14-Under	40 ft. (12.19 m)
Men	46 ft. (14.02 m)	Boys 14-Under	46 ft. (14.02 m)
Slow Pitch		Girls 16-Under	40 ft. (12.19 m)
Women	50 ft. (15.24 m)	Boys 16-Under	46 ft. (14.02 m)
Men	50 ft. (15.24 m)	Girls 18-Under	40 ft. (12.19 m)
Co-ed	50 ft. (15.24 m)	Boys 18-Under	46 ft. (14.02 m)
Super	50 ft. (15.24 m)	Slow Pitch	
16'' Slow Pitch		Girls 10-Under	35 ft. (10.67 m)
Women	38 ft. (11.58 m)	Boys 10-Under	35 ft. (10.67 m)
Men	38 ft. (11.58 m)	Girls 12-Under	40 ft. (12.19 m)
		Boys 12-Under	40 ft. (12.19 m)
		Girls 14-Under	46 ft. (14.02 m)
		Boys 14-Under	46 ft. (14.02 m)
		Girls 16-Under	46 ft. (14.02 m)
		Boys 16-Under	46 ft. (14.02 m)
		Girls 18-Under	46 ft. (14.02 m)
		Boys 18-Under	**50 ft. (15.24 m)**

NOTE: If the base distances or the pitching distance is found to be at the wrong dimensions during the course of the game, correct the error and continue playing the game.

Sec. 4. FOR THE LAYOUT OF THE DIAMOND, REFER TO DRAWING SHOWING OFFICIAL DIMENSIONS OF SOFTBALL DIAMOND. THIS SECTION SERVES AS AN EXAMPLE FOR LAYING OUT A DIAMOND WITH 60-FOOT BASES AND A 46-FOOT PITCHING DISTANCE. To determine the position of home plate, draw a line in the direction desired to lay the diamond. Drive a stake at the corner of home plate nearest the catcher. Fasten a cord to this stake and tie knots, or otherwise mark the cord, at 46 feet (14.02 m), 60 feet (18.29 m), 84 feet 10¼ inches (25.86 m), and at 120 feet (36.58 m).

Place the cord (without stretching) along the direction line and place a stake at the 46-foot (14.02 m) marker — this will be the front line at the middle of the pitcher's plate. Along the same line, drive a stake at the 84-foot 10¼ inch (25.68 m) marker. This will be the center of second base. For the 65-foot base distance, this line will be 91 feet 11 inches (28.07 m).

Place the 120-foot (36.58 m) marker at the center of second base, and taking hold of the cord at the 60-foot (18.29 m) marker, walk to the right of the direction line until the cord is taut and drive a stake at the 60-foot (18.29 m) marker. This will be the outside corner of first base, and the cord will now form the lines to first and second bases. Again, holding the cord at the 60-foot (18.29 m) marker, walk across the field and, in like manner, mark the outside corner of third base. Home plate, first base, and third base are wholly inside the diamond.

To check the diamond, place the home plate end of the cord at the first base stake and the 120-foot (36.58 m) marker at third base. The 60-foot (18.29 m) marker should now check at home plate and second base.

In laying out a 65-foot base path diamond, follow the same procedure with the following substitute dimensions: 65-foot (19.81 m), 130-foot (39.62 m), and 91-feet 11 inches (28.07 m).

Check all distances with a steel tape whenever possible.

a. **THE 3-FOOT (0.91 m) LINE** is drawn parallel to and 3 feet (0.91 m) from the baseline, starting at a point halfway between home plate and first base.
b. **THE BATTER'S ON-DECK CIRCLE** is a 5-foot (1.52 m) circle (2½-foot [0.76 m] radius) placed adjacent to the end of players' bench or dugout area closest to home plate.
c. **THE BATTER'S BOX**, one on each side of home plate, shall measure 3 feet (0.91 m) by 7 feet (2.13 m). The inside lines of the batter's box shall be 6 inches (15.24 cm) from home plate. The front line of the box shall be 4 feet (1.22 m) in front of a line drawn through the center of home plate. The lines are considered as being within the batter's box.
d. **THE CATCHER'S BOX** shall be 10 feet (3.05 m) in length from the rear outside corners of the batters' boxes and shall be 8 feet 5 inches (2.57 m) wide.
e. **EACH COACH'S BOX IS BEHIND A LINE 15 FEET (4.57 m) LONG DRAWN OUTSIDE THE DIAMOND.** The line is parallel to and 8 feet (2.44 m) from the first and third baselines, extended from the bases toward home plate.

f. **THE PITCHER'S PLATE** shall be permanently attached to the ground at distances indicated in Rule 2, Sec. 3. (FP ONLY) There shall be a 16-foot (4.88 m) circle, 8 feet (2.44 m) in radius, drawn from the pitcher's plate. The lines drawn around the pitcher's plate are considered inside the circle.

RULE 3. EQUIPMENT

Sec. 1. THE OFFICIAL BAT.

a. Shall be made of one piece of hardwood, or formed from a block of wood consisting of two or more pieces of wood bonded together with an adhesive in such a way that the grain direction of all pieces is essentially parallel to the length of the bat.
b. Shall be metal, plastic, graphite, carbon, magnesium, fiberglass, ceramic, or any other composite material approved by the ASA. Any new composite construction bat must be reviewed and approved by the ASA.
c. May be laminated, but must contain only wood or adhesive and have a clear finish (if finished).
d. Shall be round or three-sided and shall be smooth. If the barrel end has knurled finish, the maximum surface roughness is no more than 250 if measured by a profilometer or 4/1000 if measured by a spectrograph.
e. Shall not be more than 34 inches (87.0 cm) long nor exceed 38 ounces (1100.0 g) in weight.
f. If round, shall not be more than 2¼ inches (6.0 cm) in diameter at its largest part; and if three-sided, shall not exceed 2¼ inches (6.0 cm) on the hitting surface. A tolerance of 1/32 inch (0.80 mm) is permitted to allow for expansion on the round bat.
g. If metal, may be angular.
h. Shall not have exposed rivets, pins, rough or sharp edges, or any form of exterior fastener that would present a hazard. A metal bat shall be free of burrs.
i. If metal, shall not have a wooden handle.
j. Shall have a safety grip of cork, tape (not smooth, plastic-type), or composition material. The safety grip shall not be less than 10 inches (25.0 cm) long and shall not extend more than 15 inches (40.0 cm) from the small end of the bat. Any molded finger-formed grip made by the bat manufacturer, if used, must be permanently attached to the bat or attached to the bat with safety tape, and must be approved by the Equipment Standards Committee. NOTE: The "Trigger-Grip" was approved in 1991. Resin, pine tar, or spray substances placed on the safety grip to enhance the grip are permissible on the grip only. NOTE: Tape applied to any bat must be continuously spiral. It does not have to be a solid layer of tape. It may not exceed two layers.
k. If metal, and not made of one-piece construction with the barrel end closed, shall have a rubber or vinyl plastic insert firmly secured at the large end of the bat.
l. Shall have a safety knob of a minimum of ¼ inch protruding at a 90-degree angle from the handle. It may be molded, lathed, welded, or permanently fastened. A "flare" or "cone" grip attached to the bat will be considered an altered bat.
m. Shall be marked *OFFICIAL SOFTBALL* by the manufacturer. If the words *OFFICIAL SOFTBALL* cannot be read due to wear and tear on the bat, the bat should be declared legal if it is legal in all other aspects.

NOTE: Softball bats used in ASA championship tournament play must be approved by the Equipment Standards Committee. Bats with special design features to enhance hit distance will not be allowed. Manufacturers must submit all new designed bats to the ASA Equipment Standards Committee for approval prior to sales.

Sec. 2. WARM-UP BATS. No more than two official softball bats, one ASA approved warm-up bat, or a combination of the two — not to exceed two — may be used by the on-deck batter in the on-deck circle. The WARM-UP BAT should meet the following requirements to be approved: a) stamped with ¼-inch letters *WB* on either end of the bat or marked in 1-inch letters the words *Warm-Up Bat Only* on the barrel end of the bat; b) a minimum weight of 48 ounces (1360.0 g); c) a minimum barrel diameter of 2½ inches (6.0 cm); d) have a safety grip of at least 10 inches (25.0 cm) and no more than 15 inches (40.0 cm) extended from the knob; and/or e) be of one-piece construction or a one-piece permanently assembled bat approved by the Equipment Standards Committee.

Sec. 3. THE OFFICIAL SOFTBALL.

a. Shall be a regular, smooth-seamed, flat-surfaced ball with concealed stitches.
b. Shall have a center core made of either No. 1 quality long fibre kapok, a mixture of cork and rubber, a polyurethane mixture, or other materials approved by the ASA.
c. May be hand or machine-wound with a fine quality twisted yarn and covered with latex or rubber cement.
d. Shall have a cover cemented to the ball by application of cement to the underside of the cover and sewn with waxed thread of cotton or linen. If the cover is molded, it may be a) bonded to the core or b) be of the same composition as the core. Either molded type must have an authentic facsimile of stitching as approved by the ASA.
e. Shall have a cover of chrome-tanned, top-grain horsehide or cowhide; synthetic material; or other materials approved by the ASA.
f. The 12-inch (30.0 cm) ball shall be between 11-7/8 inches (30.0 cm) and 12-1/8 inches (31.0 cm) in circumference and shall weigh between 6¼ ounces (180.0 g) and 7 ounces (200.0 g). The smooth-seamed style shall not have fewer than 88 stitches in each cover, sewn by the two-needle method, or with an authentic facsimile of stitching as approved by the ASA.
g. The 11-inch (27.0 cm) ball shall be between 10-7/8 inches (27.0 cm) and 11-1/8 inches (28.0 cm) in circumference and shall weigh between 5-7/8 ounces (165.0 g) and 6-1/8 ounces (175.0 g). The smooth-seamed style shall not have fewer than 80 stitches in each cover, sewn by the two-needle method, or with an authentic facsimile of stitching as approved by the ASA.
h. The white-stitch 12-inch ball shall be used in the following ASA play: men's and women's fast pitch, boys and girls Junior Olympic 12-, 14-, 16-, and 18-under fast pitch; and boys 14-, 16-, and 18-under slow pitch. It must have a COR of .50 or under and be so marked.
i. The white-stitch 11-inch ball shall be used in the following ASA play: boys and girls Junior Olympic 10-under fast pitch. It must have a COR of .50 and under and show the ASA logo.
j. The red-stitch *(and/or red indelible stamping as approved by the ASA)* 12-inch ball with a COR of .47 and under shall be used in the following ASA Play: Adult men's slow pitch and co-ed slow pitch (male batters only). It must be marked MSP-47 and show the ASA logo.
k. The red-stitch *(and/or red indelible stamping as approved by the ASA)* 11-inch ball with a COR of .47 and under shall be used in the following ASA Play: Women's slow pitch, co-ed slow pitch (women batters only), boys Junior Olympic 10-under and 12-under slow pitch and all girls Junior Olympic slow pitch. It must be marked GWSP-47 and show the ASA logo.
l. Softballs used in ASA play must meet standards set by the ASA Equipment Standards Committee as shown below and must be stamped with the ASA logo.

THE OFFICIAL SOFTBALL SPECIFICATIONS ARE AS FOLLOWS:

SOFTBALL	THREAD COLOR	MINIMUM SIZE	MAXIMUM SIZE	MINIMUM SIZE	MAXIMUM SIZE	MARKING
12-inch FP (30.0 cm)	white	11 7/8 in 30.0 cm	12 1/8 in 31.0 cm	6¼ oz 180.0 g	7 oz 200.0 g	ASA Logo
12-inch SP (30.0 cm)	red	11 7/8 in 30.0 cm	12 1/8 in 31.0 cm	6¼ oz 180.0 g	7 oz 200.0 g	MSP-47 ASA Logo
16-inch SP (41.0) cm)	white	15 7/8 in 40.0 cm	16 1/8 in 41.0 cm	9 oz 225.0 g	10 oz 283.0 g	ASA Logo
11-inch (27.0 cm)	red	10 7/8 in 27.0 cm	11 1/8 in 28.0 cm	5 7/8 oz 165.0 g	6 1/8 oz 175.0 g	GWSP-47 ASA Logo
11-inch (27.0 cm)	white	10 7/8 in 27.0 cm	11 1/8 in 28.0 cm	5 7/8 oz 165.0 g	6 1/8 oz 175.0 g	ASA logo

Sec. 4. THE HOME PLATE SHALL BE MADE OF RUBBER OR OTHER SUITABLE MATERIAL(S). It shall be a five-sided figure, 17 inches (43.18 cm) wide across the edge facing the pitcher. The sides shall be parallel to the inside lines of the batter's box and shall be 8½ inches (21.59 cm) long. The sides of the point facing the catcher shall be 12 inches (30.48 cm) long.

a. (SLOW PITCH 55-OVER) A second home plate shall be placed adjacent to the right handed-batter's box. (Refer to Rule 8, Section 10d).

Sec. 5. THE PITCHER'S PLATE shall be of wood or rubber, 24 inches (60.96 cm) long and 6 inches (15.24 cm) wide. The top of the plate shall be level with the ground. The front line of the plate shall be the prescribed pitching distances from the back point of home plate. (Refer to PITCHING DISTANCES chart in Rule 2, Sec. 3.)

Sec. 6. THE BASES. OTHER THAN HOME PLATE SHALL BE 15 INCHES (38.10 cm) SQUARE, MADE OF CANVAS OR OTHER SUITABLE MATERIAL(S), AND NOT MORE THAN 5 INCHES (12.70 cm) IN THICKNESS. The bases should be securely fastened in position.

a. The double base is approved for use at first base. This base is 15 by 30 inches and made of canvas or other suitable material(s). Half the base is white (secured in fair territory), and half is orange (secured in foul territory). It should not be more than 5 inches (12.70 cm) in thickness.

NOTE: The following rules apply to the double base:
1) A batted ball hitting the white portion is declared fair, and a batted ball hitting the orange portion is declared foul.
2) Both white and orange portions of the base are treated equally for the offense and the defense.
REFER TO POINTS OF EMPHASIS.

b. (SLOW PITCH 55-OVER) The double first base shall be used in this division of play.

SOFTBALL GLOVE SPECIFICATIONS

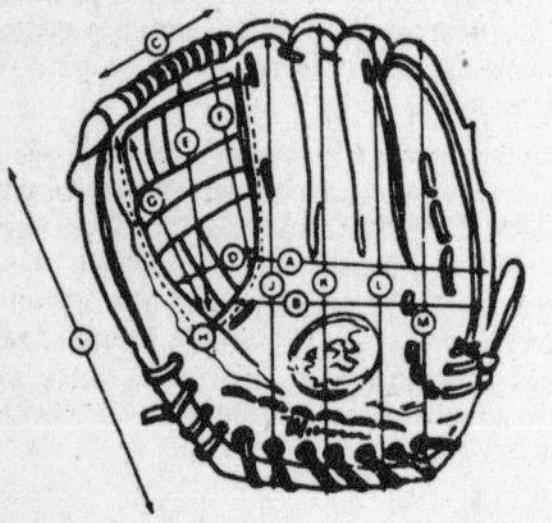

(A) Palm width .... 8 in.
(B) Palm width .... 8½ in.
(C) Top opening of web ...... 5 in.
(D) Bottom opening of web . 4½ in.
(E) Web top to bottom ..... 7¼ in.
(F) First finger crotch seam . 7½ in.
(G) Thumb crotch seam ... 7½ in.
(H) Crotch seam .... 17½ in.
(I) Thumb top to bottom Edge .... 9¼ in.
(J) First finger top to bottom edge .... 14 in.
(K) Second finger top to Bottom edge .... 13¼ in.
(L) Third finger top to bottom edge .... 12¼ in.
(M) Fourth finger top to bottom edge .... 11 in.

Sec. 7. GLOVES MAY BE WORN BY ANY PLAYER, BUT MITTS MAY BE USED ONLY BY THE CATCHER AND FIRST BASEMAN. No top lacing, webbing, or other device between the thumb and body of the glove or mitt worn by a first baseman or catcher, or a glove worn by any fielder, shall be more than 5 inches (12.70 cm) in length. The pitcher's glove shall be of one solid color other than white or grey. Multicolored gloves are acceptable for all other players. Gloves with white or grey circles on the outside, giving the appearance of a ball, are illegal for all players.

Sec. 8. SHOES MUST BE WORN BY ALL PLAYERS. A SHOE SHALL BE CONSIDERED OFFICIAL IF IT IS MADE WITH EITHER CANVAS OR LEATHER UPPERS OR SIMILAR MATERIAL(S). The soles may be either smooth or have soft or hard rubber cleats. Ordinary metal sole and heel plates may be used if the spikes on the plates do not extend more than 3/4 of an inch (1.91 cm) from the sole or heel of the shoe. Shoes with rounded metal spikes are illegal. No shoes with detachable cleats that screw ON are allowed; however, shoes with detachable cleats that screw INTO the shoe are allowed.

J.O./CO-ED PLAY: No metal spikes are allowed in any division of J.O. or co-ed play. No hard plastic or polyurethane spikes similar to metal sole and heel plates are allowed in any division of J.O. or co-ed play.

PLAY — *Adult players from Team B are wearing (a) golf shoes, (b) track shoes, (c) metal baseball spikes, (d) coaches' shoes with rippled rubber soles. RULING — (a) and (b) Illegal; (c) and (d) Legal.*

Sec. 9. MASKS, BODY PROTECTORS, AND SHIN GUARDS.

a. (FP ONLY) Masks with throat protectors must be worn by adult catchers, and Junior Olympic catchers must wear a mask, throat protector, and helmet. An extended wire protector may be worn in lieu of a throat protector attached to the mask. NOTE: Any player warming up a Junior Olympic pitcher at any location within the confines of the playing field shall wear a mask and throat protector.

b. (SP ONLY) Junior Olympic catchers must wear an approved batter's helmet with ear flaps, or the catcher's helmet and mask.

c. (FP ONLY) Junior Olympic catchers must wear shin guards and body protectors.

PLAY (1) — *Adult catcher refuses to wear a mask in (a) slow pitch, (b) fast pitch. RULING — (a) Legal, (b) Illegal. Catcher must wear a mask in fast pitch, and all J.O. catchers must wear masks with helmets.*

PLAY (2) — *(FP ONLY) A catcher refuses to comply with umpire's order to wear a mask. RULING — Forfeited game shall be declared by the umpire if no one else will wear mask and catch.*

NOTE: NO EQUIPMENT SHALL BE LEFT LYING ON THE FIELD EITHER IN FAIR OR FOUL TERRITORY. (See Rule 8, Sec. 5g-Play 4.)

Sec. 10. UNIFORM. All players on a team shall wear uniforms alike in color, trim, and style. Coaches must be neatly attired and dressed alike or in team uniform and in accordance with the color code of the team.

a. HEADWEAR.
1. (FP Male) All ball caps are mandatory and must be alike. They must be worn properly.
2. (SP Male and Female and FP Female) Ball caps, visors, and headbands are optional for all players. Players are not required to wear headwear, but if worn, all headwear must be of the same type (i.e., all caps, all visors, or all headbands) and must be worn properly. Handkerchiefs do not qualify as headbands and cannot be worn around the head or neck. NOTE: Plastic visors are not allowed as headwear.

PLAY (1) — *A female team (or slow pitch male team) has three players wearing caps, but the remaining players do not wear anything on their heads. RULING — Legal if the three caps are alike. All female or male slow pitch players do not have to wear caps. If caps are worn, however, they may not be mixed with headbands or visors.*

PLAY (2) — *Two female players wear caps, and the remaining players wear similar-colored headbands. RULING — Illegal. Either caps or headbands may be worn, but not both.*

PLAY (3) — *In co-ed play, 4 males wear caps, 1 does not, 2 females have headbands, and 3 do not. RULING — Illegal. It is permissable for players not to wear headbands or caps, but they may not be mixed. The rest of the uniform should be similar (i.e., all players in shorts or all in long pants, the same jerseys and leggings, etc.).*

b. PANTS/SLIDING PANTS. All player pants shall be either all long or all short in style. Players may wear a uniform, solid-colored pair of sliding pants. It is not mandatory that all players wear sliding pants, but if more than one player wear them, they must be alike in color and style. No player may wear ragged, frayed, or slit legs on exposed sliding pants.

c. UNDERSHIRTS. Players may wear a uniform, solid-colored undershirt (it may be white). It is not mandatory that all players wear an undershirt if one player wears one, but those that are worn must be alike. No player may wear ragged, frayed, or slit sleeves on exposed undershirts.

d. NUMBERS. An Arabic number of contrasting color at least 6 inches (15.24 cm) high, must be worn on the back of all uniform shirts. No players on the same team may wear identical numbers. (Numbers *3* and *03* are examples of identical numbers.) Players without numbers will not be permitted to play. If duplicate numbers exist, only one of the players may play at a time.

PLAY (4) — *Player F1 wears (a) uniform number 6 on the back of his jersey, (b) uniform number 00 on the back of his jersey, (c) no uniform number on the jersey but number 5 on the pants, (d) no uniform number on the back of the jersey but a 2-inch number on the front, (e) no uniform number at all. RULING — Legal in (a) and (b), not legal in (c), (d), or (e).*

PLAY (5) — *Player F1 (Jones) was listed in the scorebook with the wrong number and (a) had his name on the jersey, (b) had no name on the jersey. RULING — Correct the number in the scorebook in either case and resume play. There is no penalty.*

e. HELMETS. All adult fast pitch and Junior Olympic fast and slow pitch offensive players (TO INCLUDE THE ON-DECK BATTER) must properly wear batting helmets of similar color with double ear flaps. J.O. players acting as coaches in the coaches' box(es) must wear a batting helmet. All helmets must be approved by the National Operating Committee on Standards for Athletic Equipment (NOCSAE). PENALTY: Failure to wear the batting helmet when ordered to do so by the umpire shall cause said player to be ejected from the game. Deliberately wearing the helmet improperly or deliberately removing the helmet during a live ball play and seen by the umpire as a deliberate act, shall cause the violator to be declared out immediately. The ball remains alive. EXCEPTION: Modified pitch players are not required to wear when playing offense.

NOTE: Calling a runner out for removing a helmet does not remove force play situations.

Pitchers and catchers may wear batting helmets. Other than pitchers and catchers, no other defensive player may wear a helmet in adult and J.O. play except for medical purposes.

NOTE: Catcher helmets at the present time do not have NOCSAE standards, and no stamp will be required on these helmets.

PLAY — *B4 hits an out-of-the-park home run and as he passes third base removes his helmet in a fast pitch game. The plate umpire calls B4 out. RULING — Although the rule reads that baserunners are to be called out if they remove the helmet intentionally, the intent of this rule is to prevent the baserunner from getting hit with a thrown bal. When the ball has been hit over the fence for a home run, no play will be made on any baserunner, until the plate umpire throws another ball into the game. Baserunners should not be called out for removing the helmet on a home-run ball that is hit out of the park.*

f. CASTS. Plaster or other hard substances in their final form may not be worn during the game. Any exposed metal may be considered legal if covered by soft material and taped.

g. JEWELRY. Exposed jewelry, which is judged by the umpire to be dangerous, may not be worn during the game. NOTE: Players must be asked to remove jewelry if judged to be dangerous. If they fail to do so, the player is ejected from the game.

RULE 4. PLAYERS & SUBSTITUTES

Sec. 1. A TEAM SHALL CONSIST OF:

a. Fast Pitch - 9 players.
b. Fast Pitch with a designated player - 10 players.
c. Slow Pitch - 10 players.
d. Slow Pitch with an extra player - 11 players.
e. Male rosters shall include only male players, and female rosters shall include only female players.
f. Co-Ed - 10 players (5 male and 5 female).
g. Co-Ed Slow Pitch with extra players — 12 players (6 male and 6 female). NOTE: If the EP is used in Co-Ed, 12 players must be used. It is not permissible to use 11 players because of the alternate batters.
h. A team must have the required number of players present to start or continue a game. PENALTY: The game is forfeited (See Rule 5, Sec. 3g(7)). NOTE: Players listed on the starting lineup and not available at game time may be substituted for and re-entered under the re-entry rule. The proper number of players must be in the team area at game time.

Sec. 2. PLAYERS' POSITIONS SHALL BE DESIGNATED AS FOLLOWS:

a. Fast Pitch: Pitcher, catcher, first baseman, second baseman, third baseman, shortstop, left fielder, center fielder, and right fielder.

b. Fast Pitch with a designated player: Same as Fast Pitch in paragraph *a* above, plus a designated player.
c. Slow Pitch: Same as Fast Pitch in paragraph *a* above, plus a short fielder.
d. Slow Pitch with an extra player: Same as Slow Pitch in paragraph *c* above, plus an extra player who bats.

NOTE: Players of the team in the field must be stationed anywhere in fair territory, except the catcher who must be in the catcher's box, and the pitcher who must be in a legal pitching position at the start of each pitch. When a pitch is delivered without all defensive players in fair territory, an illegal pitch shall be declared.

e. Co-Ed defensive positioning shall include 2 males and 2 females in the outfield, 2 males and 2 females in the infield, and 1 male and 1 female in the pitcher-catcher positions. Once determining positions, the players must be stationed anywhere on fair ground, except the catcher as indicated in the "NOTE" above.

Sec. 3. DESIGNATED PLAYER (FP ONLY)

a. A designated player, referred to as a "DP," may be used for any player, provided it is made known prior to the start of the game and his name is indicated on the lineup sheet or score sheet as one of the nine hitters in the batting order. The starting DP may re-enter one time, as long as he returns to the position in the batting order that he occupied when he left the game.
b. The starting player listed as the DP must remain in the same position in the batting order for the entire game. The DP and his substitute or replacement may never play offense at the same time.
c. The DP may be substituted for at any time, either by a pinch-hitter, pinch-runner, or the defensive player for whom he is hitting. If the starting DP is replaced on offense by the person for whom he is hitting (number 10 on the batting order), or by a substitute, the DP is considered to have left the game, and he may re-enter one time, as long as he returns to his original position in the batting order. NOTE: a) If replaced by the person playing defense only, this reduces the number of players from ten to nine. If the DP does not re-enter, the game may legally end with nine players, b) If the DP re-enters, he may play offense and defense (continue with nine players), or he may bat in his original spot in the batting order, and the defensive player returns to the number 10 position and plays defense only once again. Penalty: Placing the defensive player only (number 10 on the batting order) into the first nine positions for someone other than the original DP is considered an illegal re-entry. The manager and the defensive player only are ejected.
d. The DP may play defense at any position. Should the DP play defense for a player other than the one for whom he is batting, that player will continue to bat but not play defense, and is not considered to have left the game. The DP may play defense for the person for whom he is hitting (number 10 in batting order), and that person is considered to have left the game, reducing the number of players from ten to nine. The person being hit for may re-enter the game one time, either in the number 10 spot in the batting order or in the DP's position in the batting order. NOTE: a) If returning to the #10 position, he will again play defense only but may play any defensive position, b) If returning in the DP's position, he will play offense and defense, and there will be only nine players on the batting order.

NOTE: The name of the player for whom the DP is batting will be placed in the tenth position in the scorebook.

PLAY (1) — In the fifth inning Jones comes into the game as a DP and is placed at the end of the batting order. RULING — Illegal. The DP must be announced prior to the start of the game and his name entered on the starting lineup. If one pitch is thrown to Jones, he is considered an illegal substitute for the player listed number 1 on the batting order.

PLAY (2) — At the beginning of the game, Jones is put into the lineup as a DP for Smith. In the third inning Smith is injured and has to leave the game. Jones replaces Smith as shortstop. RULING — Legal. The game may continue with nine players.

PLAY (3) — Jones begins the game at second base but does not bat. In the fourth inning he takes the place of Smith as the DP. RULING — Legal. The role of the DP is terminated until Smith (or Smith's substitute) re-enters the game.

PLAY (4) — Jones is the listed DP and is batting third. Smith, the third baseman, is listed as the DEFO. Brown, the second baseman, is batting seventh. In the third inning Jones plays defense for Brown. In the sixth inning, the manager wants Smith to bat and inserts him for Brown, the temporary DP, who was batting only. RULING — Illegal. Brown was not the starting DP. Smith must bat for Jones if the manager wants him to bat. The umpire should correct this at the time of the change. If not detected at that time, the violation will be treated as an illegal substitution when brought to the attention of the umpire by the offended team after the first legal or illegal pitch. The starter can report and re-enter legally.

Sec. 4. EXTRA PLAYER (SP ONLY)

a. An extra player, referred to as an "EP," is optional, but if one is used, it must be made known prior to the start of the game and be listed on the scoring sheet in the regular batting order. If the EP is used, he must be used the entire game. Failure to complete the game with the EP results in forfeiture of the game.
b. The EP must remain in the same position in the batting order for the entire game.
c. If an EP is used, all 11 must bat and any 10 may play defense. Defensive positions may be changed, but the batting order must remain the same.
d. The EP may be substituted for at any time. The substitute must be a player who has not yet been in the game. The starting EP may re-enter.
e. The EP is used in Co-Ed, all 12 must be, and any 10 — 5 male and 5 female — may play defense. Defensive positions may be changed as long as the following ratio is used: 2 male/2 female in the outfield, 2 male/2 female in the infield, and 1 male/1 female as pitcher/catcher. The batting order must remain the same throughout the game.
f. (55-Over Only). Two extra players may be designated at any place in the batting order. The EPs may enter a game on defense at any time, but must remain in the same batting order.

Sec. 5. RE-ENTRY — Any of the starting players, including a DP (FP ONLY) or an EP (SP ONLY), may be withdrawn and re-entered once, provided players occupy the same batting positions whenever in the lineup.

EXCEPTION: When the defensive player bats for the DP (FP ONLY), the DP is temporarily eliminated.

NOTE: The original player and the substitute(s) may not be in the lineup at the same time. If a manager removes a substitute from the game and re-enters the same substitute later in the game, this is considered an illegal re-entry.

a. Violation of the re-entry rule results in the ejection of both the manager and the illegal player when the violation is brought to the attention of the umpire by the offended team.
b. Violation of the re-entry rule is handled as a protest which may be made anytime DURING THE GAME. The protest need not be made prior to the next pitch as described in Rule 11, Sec. 4; however, all play that occurred while the illegal re-entry was in the game will stand.

NOTE: If the re-entry violation also violates the unreported substitute ruling (Rule 4, Sec. 7a), those penalties would also be in effect.

PLAY (1) — Brown replaces Carter, a starting player, in the third inning. Carter re-enters the game in the sixth inning for Green, another starting player. Carter singles, and the opponents bring to the attention of the umpire that Carter's re-entry was not reported. RULING — This is a violation of the re-entry rule since Carter did not replace his substitute. Both Carter and his manager are ejected from the game.

PLAY (2) — In the top half of the first inning with two outs, R1 on first base, B4 (Smith) is announced on the PA system. Just then the manager decides to substitute Jones for Smith. Jones strikes out. In the third inning Smith, who was announced in the first inning, pinch-hits for Jones. RULING — Legal. Members of the starting lineup may be withdrawn and re-entered one time, provided they occupy the same batting positions they held when originally in the lineup.

Sec. 6. A STARTING PLAYER SHALL BE OFFICIAL WHEN THE LINE-UP IS INSPECTED AND APPROVED BY THE PLATE UMPIRE AND TEAM MANAGER AT THE PRE-GAME MEETING. The names may be entered on the official score sheet in advance of this meeting. However, in case of injury or illness, changes can be made at the pre-game meeting. A substitute may take the place of a player whose name is in his team's batting order. The following regulations govern the substitution of players:

a. The manager or team representative of the team making the substitution shall immediately notify the plate umpire at the time a substitute enters. The plate umpire shall then report the change to the scorer prior to the next pitch. If the violation is discovered prior to a pitch being made (legal or illegal), there is no penalty, and the illegal substitute shall be declared legal.

The use of an illegal substitute or an ineligible player is handled as a protest by the offended team. All other substitutes are considered in the game as described in Rule 4, Sec. 6b. If the team manager or player in violation informs the umpire prior to the offended team's protest, there is no violation regardless of how long the player or players were illegally in the game.

The illegal substitute is considered in the game if a pitch has been made (legal or illegal). OFFENSE: (1) If the illegal player is discovered by the defense after one legal or illegal pitch has been thrown while he is at bat, and before the offensive manager, coach, or player in violation informs the umpire, he is declared ineligible, and a legal substitute assumes the ball and strike count. Any advance of baserunners while the illegal batter is at bat is legal. (2) If the illegal player is discovered by the defense after he has completed his turn at bat and prior to the next legal or illegal pitch, or before the defensive team has left the field; and before the offensive manager, coach, or player in violation informs the umpire; the illegal player is called out, is ruled ineligible, and any advance of baserunners as a result of obstruction, an error, a hit batsman (FP), a walk, or a basehit is nullified. (3) If the illegal player is discovered by the defense after he has completed his turn at bat and after the next legal or illegal pitch, or after the defensive team has left the field; and before the offensive manager, coach, or player in violation informs the umpire; the illegal player is ruled ineligible and any advance by baserunners while the illegal batter was at bat is legal. DEFENSE: (1) If the illegal player is discovered by the offense after he makes a play and prior to the next legal or illegal pitch, or before the defensive team has left the field; or before the defensive manager, coach, or player in violation informs the umpire; the offensive team has the option of taking the result of the play, or having the last batter rebat and assume the ball and strike count he had prior to the discovery of the illegal player, with each baserunner returning to the base at which he was prior to the play. The illegal player is ruled ineligible. (2) If the illegal player is discovered by the offense after a legal or illegal pitch to the next batter, or after the defensive manager, coach, or player in violation informs the umpire; all play(s) stand, but the illegal player is ruled ineligible.

NOTE: When the illegal substitute is ruled ineligible, he is removed from the game. If he is discovered participating again after his removal, the game is declared a forfeit (Rule 1, Sec. 36).

PLAY (1) — Jones, a legal substitute, enters the game unreported in the third inning. In the fifth inning the opponents report this to the umpire. RULING: The player (Jones) is immediately removed and is declared ineligible. All play by or on Jones is legal. A legal substitute must be reported into the game.

PLAY (2) — Smith re-enters the game unreported in the fourth inning for his substitute. After he hits the ball and reaches first base safely, it is detected by the opponents and reported to the umpire. RULING: Smith is called out, ruled ineligible, and a legal substitute must enter the game. If a substitute is not available, the game is forfeited.

b. Substitute players will be considered in the game when reported to the plate umpire. A player will not violate the substitution rule until one legal or illegal pitch has been thrown.
c. Any player may be removed from the game during any dead ball.

NOTE: The pitcher no longer has to pitch until the first batter facing him has completed his turn at bat, the side has been retired, or he has been removed from the game. A fast pitch pitcher returning in the same half inning will not receive warm-up pitches.

PLAY (1) — Jones is the starting pitcher. In the top of the third inning, Smith bats for Jones. In the bottom of the third, Jones returns to pitch. RULING: Legal.

PLAY (2) — Pitcher Jones walks B3 and is replaced by Smith. The offense substitutes B11 for B4, and before Smith throws one pitch, (a) Jones, the starting pitcher, re-enters, (b) Brown is substituted for Smith. RULING: Legal in both situations.

d. A player who has been declared ineligible but has not been ejected from the game may serve as a base coach.

RULE 5. THE GAME

Sec. 1. THE CHOICE OF THE FIRST OR LAST BAT IN THE INNING SHALL BE DECIDED BY A TOSS OF A COIN, UNLESS OTHERWISE STATED IN THE RULES OF THE ORGANIZATION UNDER WHICH THE SCHEDULE OF GAMES IS BEING PLAYED.

Sec. 2. THE FITNESS OF THE GROUND FOR A GAME SHALL BE DECIDED SOLELY BY THE PLATE UMPIRE.

Sec. 3. A REGULATION GAME SHALL CONSIST OF SEVEN INNINGS.

a. A full 7 innings need not be played if the team second at bat scores more runs in 6½ innings, or before the third out in the last of the seventh inning.

b. A game that is tied at the end of seven innings shall be continued by playing additional innings; or until one side has scored more runs than the other at the end of a complete inning; or until the team second at bat has scored more runs in its half of the inning before the third out is made.

c. A game called by the umpire shall be regulation if five or more complete innings have been played, or if the team second at bat has scored more runs in four or more innings than the other team has scored in five or more innings. The umpire is empowered to call a game at any time because of darkness, rain, fire, panic, or other causes which place the patrons or players in peril. For games called prior to five complete innings, see Sec. 3d.

PLAY — *At the end of the fourth inning, the score is H1 and V2. There is no score in the first half of the fifth, but in the last half H scores: (a) one run; (b) two runs. In either case the game is called because of rain with only one or two outs. RULING — In either case it is a regulation game. In (a) it is a tie game, but all records count. In (b) H is the winner.*

d. Games that are not considered either regulation, or regulation tie games, shall be resumed at the exact point where they were stopped. (For ASA championship tournament play, see ASA Procedural Code 9.01[a]).

e. A regulation tie game shall be declared if the score is equal when the game is called at the end of five or more complete innings, or if the team second at bat has equaled the score of the first team at bat in the incomplete inning.

PLAY — *In the last half of the sixth inning, with R1, R2, and R3 on third, second, and first bases respectively, B4 hits a home run, tying the score 6-6. It then begins to rain heavily and eventually forces the umpire to call the game. RULING — The game ends in a 6-6 tie.*

f. These provisions do not apply to any acts on the part of players, coaches, managers, team representatives, or spectators which might call for forfeiture of the game. The umpire may forfeit the game if attacked physically by any team member or spectator.

g. A forfeited game shall be declared by the umpire in favor of the team not at fault in the following cases:

(1) If a team fails to appear on the field or, being on the field, refuses to begin a game for which it is scheduled or assigned, or within a time set for forfeitures by the organization which the team represents.

(2) If one side refuses to continue to play after the game has begun, unless the game has been suspended or terminated by the umpire.

PLAY — *A game is called after seven complete innings of play because the manager of the visiting team no longer wishes to play. RULING — If weather permits, the game shall not be terminated. The umpire shall forfeit the game to the home team by a score of 7-0.*

(3) If, after play has been suspended by the umpire, one side fails to resume playing within 2 minutes after play ball has been declared by the umpire.

(4) If a team employs tactics noticeably designed to delay or to hasten the game.

(5) If, after warning by the umpire, any one of the rules of the game is willfully violated.

(6) If the order for the ejection of a player is not obeyed within 1 minute.

(7) If, because of the removal or ejection of a player or players from the game by the umpire, or for any reason there are fewer than 9 (Fast Pitch), 10 (Fast Pitch with DP), 10 (Slow Pitch), 11 (Slow Pitch with EP), or 12 (Co-Ed Slow Pitch with 2 EPs) on either team.

EXCEPTION: If a team starts the game with a DP (FP ONLY) and the defensive player bats for the DP (Rule 4, Sec. 3c), the team may continue and end the game with 9 players, or the DP may re-enter, and the team will finish with 10 players.

PLAY — *A team starts a game with 10 players (or 11 with EP) in slow pitch or 9 players (10 with DP) in fast pitch, but loses one player due to injury and has no substitute to replace the injured player. RULING — The game is forfeited to the opponent. A team may not continue a game with fewer than the number of players required to start the game.*

Sec. 4. THE WINNER OF THE GAME SHALL BE THE TEAM THAT SCORES MORE RUNS IN A REGULATION GAME.

a. The score of a called regulation game shall be the score at the end of the last complete inning, unless the team second at bat has scored an equal number of or more runs than the first team at bat in the incomplete inning. In this case the score shall be that of the incomplete inning.

b. The score of a regulation tie game shall be the tie score when the game was terminated.

c. The score of a forfeited game shall be 7-0 in favor of the team not at fault.

Sec. 5. ONE RUN SHALL BE SCORED EACH TIME A BASERUNNER LEGALLY TOUCHES FIRST BASE, SECOND BASE, THIRD BASE, AND HOME PLATE BEFORE THE THIRD OUT OF THE INNING.

Sec. 6. A RUN SHALL NOT BE SCORED IF THE THIRD OUT OF THE INNING IS A RESULT OF:

a. The batter-runner being put out before legally touching first base.

b. A baserunner being forced out due to the batter becoming a batter-runner.

NOTE: If there is no force out and a run scores prior to a baserunner being called out on a time play, the run will count.

PLAY (1) — *R1 is on third base, and R2 is on first base with two outs. Batter hits ground ball to F4 who chases R2 back toward first base and tags him (a) before R1 scores, (b) after R1 scores. RULING — Run does not count in (a) or (b) since the third out was a force out.*

PLAY (2) — *With one out and runners on second base and third base, the batter flies out for the second out. The runner on third base tags up after the catch, but the runner*

on second base does not. The runner on third base crosses the plate before an appeal is made at second base. RULING — The run will count as this is a time play and not a force out. If the runner crosses home plate after the appeal, the run would not count.

c. (FP ONLY) A baserunner leaving base before the pitcher releases the ball to the batter.
(SP ONLY) A baserunner leaving base before the pitched ball reaches home plate or before the pitched ball is batted.

Sec. 7. NO SUCCEEDING RUNNER SHALL SCORE A RUN WHEN A PRECEDING RUNNER HAS BEEN DECLARED THE THIRD OUT OF AN INNING.

PLAY (1) — *One out, R1 on third base, and R2 on second base. Batter hits a fly ball which is caught by F7. R1 tags up and leaves his base before the fly ball is touched by F7. R2 scores after tagging up and legally leaving his base. Appeal is made at third base, and umpire declares R1 out. RULING — Three outs, no runs score.*

PLAY (2) — *Two outs, R1 on third base, R2 on second base, and R3 on first base. Batter hits ball over the fence for a home run. R1 fails to touch home plate, but R2, R3, and the batter-runner touch all bases in regular order, including home plate. An appeal is made on R1 at home plate. Umpire declares R1 out. RULING — No runs score.*

Sec. 8. THERE SHALL BE ONLY ONE CHARGED CONFERENCE BETWEEN THE MANAGER AND/OR OTHER TEAM REPRESENTATIVE(S) AND THE BATTER OR BASERUNNER(S) IN AN INNING. Umpires shall not permit any such conferences in excess of one in an inning.

PENALTY: Ejection of manager or coach who insists on another charged conference.

Sec. 9. HOME RUN CLASSIFICATION (SP ONLY). A limit of over-the-fence home runs will be used in all men's and co-ed slow pitch divisions. All balls hit over the fence by a team in excess of the following limitations per game will be ruled on as shown:

Super Classification — Unlimited.

Major Classification — Twelve (12). The batter is ruled out for any in excess.

Class A Classification — Six (6). The batter is ruled out for any in excess. (Includes Major Industrial).

Class B Classification — Three (3). The batter is ruled out for any in excess. (Includes Major Church, Class A Industrial, Major co-ed, and all masters classification).

Class C Classification — One (1). The batter is ruled out for any in excess. (Includes Class A Church and Class A co-ed).

Class D Classification — None (0). The batter is ruled out for the first in excess and each subsequent player hitting a home run is declared ineligible and removed from the game.

NOTE: Any fly ball touched by a defensive player which then goes over the fence in fair territory, should be declared a four-base award and shall not be included in the total of over-the-fence home runs.

PLAY (1) — *Bases loaded with two outs. Class A slow pitch tournament with a six (6) home run limit. Team A has hit five, and batter B4 hits a home run out of the ball park. He deliberately misses 2B, and after all runs have scored, Team B appeals B4 for missing 2B. The umpire calls B4 out. Does the home run count towards the six home run limit? RULING: Yes. Whether the runner B4 intentionally or unintentionally missed 2B, the home run would count. Anytime a run scores the home run will count. If the runner B4 missed 1B, the home run would not count if the appealed out was the third of the inning.*

PLAY (2) — *Runner R1 on 2B with one out. Class A slow pitch tournament with six (6) home run limitation. Team A has hit five, and batter B4 hits a long fly ball to F8 in centerfield. F8 catches the ball and throws it over the fence so that team A will have reached the six home run limit. RULING: This would be a legal catch, and if fewer than two outs and other runners on base, the umpires should award all runners two bases for intentionally thrown ball which goes out of play. It would not count toward the home run limit.*

PLAY (3) — *A class 'A' church slow pitch team hits its second home run of the ball game, and the umpire rules the batter out. RULING: Correct call. Class 'A' church and co-ed must adhere to the class 'C' limitation of one home run per game.*

RULE 6. PITCHING REGULATIONS (Fast Pitch)

Sec. 1. PRELIMINARIES. Before starting the delivery (pitch), the pitcher shall comply with the following:

a. *(MALE ADULT AND JO BOYS ONLY)* He shall take a position with his pivot foot on the pitcher's plate and his non-pivot foot on or behind the pitcher's plate. *(FEMALE ADULT AND JO GIRLS ONLY)* She shall take a position with both feet in contact with the pitcher's plate. *(ALL)* Both feet must be on the ground within the 24-inch length of the pitcher's plate. The shoulders shall be in line with first and third bases. The hands shall be separated. The ball may be in the glove or pitching hand.

b. While in the position described in a above, he shall take the signal from the catcher.

PLAY — *Pitcher takes a signal while standing within 8 feet of the pitcher's plate but not on the plate. He then assumes legal pitching position for 1 second and pitches the ball. RULING — Illegal pitch. The pitcher must take the signal while legally in contact with the pitcher's plate.*

c. After completing b above, the pitcher shall hold the ball in both hands for not less than one (1) second and not more than ten (10) seconds before releasing it. *(MALE ADULT AND JO BOYS ONLY)* If the pitcher decides to pitch with the non-pivot foot to the rear and off the pitching plate, the backward step may be taken before, simultaneous, or after the hands are brought together. The pivot foot must remain in contact with the pitching plate at all times prior to the forward step. *(FEMALE ADULT AND JO GIRLS ONLY)* Both feet must remain in contact with the pitching plate at all times prior to the forward step.

PLAY (1) — *After taking the signal, the pitcher starts the motion and touches fingers to the glove, but does not stop the movement while performing a windmill delivery. RULING — An illegal pitch should be called. The pitcher must bring the two hands together somewhere in front of the body.*

PLAY (2) — The pitcher stands with two feet on the pitching rubber and takes the signal. He then steps or slides back with the non-pivot foot (a) while his hands are separated, (b) while his hands are together. RULING — Legal in male, illegal in female deliveries.

d. The pitcher shall not be considered in pitching position unless the catcher is in position to receive the pitch.
e. The pitcher may not take the pitching position on or near the pitcher's plate without having the ball in his possession.

NOTE: To indicate to the pitcher that he may not start the pitch, the umpire should raise one hand with the palm facing the pitcher. "NO PITCH" shall be declared if the pitcher pitches while the umpire has his hand in said position.

Sec. 2. THE PITCH starts when one hand is taken off the ball or the pitcher makes any motion that is part of his windup.

a. In the act of delivering the ball, the pitcher shall not take more than one step, which must be forward, toward the batter, and simultaneous with the delivery of the ball to the batter. (*Toward the batter* is interpreted as being within the 24-inch length of the pitcher's plate.)

PLAY — The pitcher stands on the right side of the pitcher's plate with both feet in legal contact. He takes a step with his non-pivot foot toward third base so that the entire foot lands to the right and outside the length of the pitcher's plate. RULING — Illegal Pitch.

b. Pushing off with the pivot foot from a place other than the pitcher's plate is illegal.
c. (FEMALE ADULT AND JO GIRLS ONLY) The pivot foot may remain in contact or push off and drag away from the pitching plate prior to the front foot touching the ground, as long as the pivot foot remains in contact with the ground.

NOTE: It is not a step if the pitcher slides his foot across the pitcher's plate, provided contact is maintained with the plate. Raising the foot off the pitching plate and returning it to the plate creates a rocking motion and is an illegal act.

PLAY — The pitcher stands with the non-pivot foot to the rear of the pitching plate but within the 24-inch length of the plate. He raises both arms high above his head stretching and in so doing, he pulls his pivot foot off the plate. RULING: Illegal Pitch. The pivot foot must remain in contact with the pitching plate until he pushes off during the delivery.

Sec. 3. A LEGAL DELIVERY SHALL BE A BALL WHICH IS DELIVERED TO THE BATTER WITH AN UNDERHANDED MOTION.

a. The release of the ball and follow-through of the hand and wrist must be forward and past the straight line of the body.
b. The hand shall be below the hip, and the wrist not farther from the body than the elbow.
c. The pitch is completed with a step toward the batter.
d. The catcher must remain within the lines of the catcher's box when the pitch is released.

PLAY — A pitch is delivered with the catcher outside the boundaries of the catcher's box. RULING — Illegal Pitch.

e. The catcher shall return the ball directly to the pitcher after each pitch, except after a strikeout or a putout made by the catcher.

EXCEPTION: Sec. 3e does not apply when (a) a batter becomes a batter-runner, (b) there are runners on base, or (c) a foul ball is fielded close to the foul line by the catcher who throws to any base for a possible out.

PLAY — Bases are empty, and the batter has a count of no balls and one strike. On the next pitch the batter hits a foul ball which the catcher retrieves and throws to the third baseman. RULING — A ball is awarded to the batter, and the count becomes one ball and two strikes.

f. The pitcher has twenty (20) seconds to release the next pitch after receiving the ball, or after the umpire indicates "play ball."

Sec. 4. THE PITCHER MAY USE ANY WINDUP DESIRED, PROVIDED:

a. He does not make any motion to pitch without immediately delivering the ball to the batter.
b. He does not use a rocker action in which, after having the ball in both hands in the pitching position, he removes one hand from the ball, takes a backward and forward swing, and returns the ball to both hands in front of the body.
c. He does not use a windup in which there is a stop or reversal of the forward motion.
d. He does not make two revolutions of the arm on the windmill pitch. A pitcher may drop his arm to the side and to the rear before starting the windmill motion.
e. He does not continue to wind up after taking the forward step which is simultaneous with the release of the ball.

Sec. 5. WHILE IN THE PITCHING POSITION, THE PITCHER SHALL NOT DELIBERATELY DROP, ROLL, OR BOUNCE THE BALL IN ORDER TO PREVENT THE BATTER FROM STRIKING IT. A pitchout for the purpose of intentionally walking a batter is not considered an illegal pitch. (Refer to note following Rule 8, Sec. 2c.)

Sec. 6. THE PITCHER SHALL NOT, AT ANY TIME DURING THE GAME, BE ALLOWED TO USE TAPE OR ANY OTHER FOREIGN SUBSTANCE(S) UPON THE BALL, THE PITCHING HAND, OR THE FINGERS; NOR SHALL ANY OTHER PLAYER APPLY ANY FOREIGN SUBSTANCE(S) TO THE BALL. Under the supervision and control of the umpire, powdered resin may be used to dry the hands. The pitcher shall not wear a sweatband, bracelet, or similar-type item on the wrist or forearm of the pitching arm.

PLAY — Pitcher with tape on pitching hand. RULING — Illegal. Must remove tape or be replaced.

Sec. 7. THE PITCHER SHALL NOT DELIVER A PITCH unless all defensive players, except the catcher who must be in the catcher's box, are positioned in fair territory.

NOTE: It is an illegal pitch if a fielder takes a position in the batter's line of vision or, with deliberate unsportsmanlike intent, acts in a manner to distract the batter. A pitch does not have to be released. PENALTY: The offending player shall be ejected from the game, and an illegal pitch shall be declared.

Sec. 8. THE PITCHER SHALL NOT THROW TO A BASE DURING A LIVE BALL WHILE HIS FOOT IS IN CONTACT WITH THE PITCHER'S PLATE AFTER HE HAS TAKEN THE PITCHING POSITION.

EFFECT — Sec. 8: Illegal pitch, the ball is dead, a ball is called on the batter, and all runners advance one base. If the throw from the pitcher's plate occurs during a live ball appeal play, the appeal is cancelled.

NOTE: The pitcher may remove himself from the pitching position by stepping backwards off the pitcher's plate. Stepping forward or sideways constitutes an illegal pitch.

EFFECT — Secs. 1-8: Any infraction of Secs. 1-8 is an illegal pitch, with the exception of Sec. 3e which is covered separately. The ball is dead. A ball is called on the batter. Baserunners are entitled to advance one base without liability to be put out. NOTE: If an illegal pitch hits the batter, the batter is awarded first base and all runners are awarded one base.

EXCEPTION: If the pitcher completes the delivery of the ball to the batter; and if the batter hits the ball and reaches first base safely; and if all baserunners advance at least one base on the action resulting from the batted ball; the play stands, and the illegal pitch is nullified.

NOTE: An illegal pitch shall be called immediately when it becomes illegal. If called by the plate umpire, it shall be called in a voice so that the catcher and the batter will hear it. The plate umpire will also give the delayed dead ball signal. If called by the base umpire, it shall be called so that the nearest fielder shall hear it. The base umpire shall also give the delayed dead ball signal. Failure of players to hear the call shall not void it.

Sec. 9. AT THE BEGINNING OF EACH HALF INNING, OR WHEN A PITCHER RELIEVES ANOTHER, NOT MORE THAN 1 MINUTE MAY BE USED TO DELIVER NOT MORE THAN FIVE PITCHES TO THE CATCHER OR OTHER TEAMMATE. Play shall be suspended during this time. For excessive warm-up pitches, a pitcher shall be penalized by awarding a ball to the batter for each pitch in excess of five.

PLAY — S1 replaces F1. How many throws are permitted for his warm-up? RULING — Five. The umpire is authorized to allow more throws, however, when the weather is inclement or when F1 is removed because of an injury and S1 did not have time to warm up before entering. If F1 returns to pitch in the same inning no additional warm-up pitches are allowed.

Sec. 10. NO PITCH SHALL BE DECLARED WHEN:

a. The pitcher pitches during the suspension of play.
b. The pitcher attempts a quick return of the ball before the batter has taken his position or when the batter is off balance as a result of a previous pitch.
c. A runner is called out for leaving a base prior to the pitcher releasing the pitch.
d. The pitcher pitches before a baserunner has retouched his base after a foul ball has been declared and the ball is dead.

EFFECT — Sec. 10a-d: The ball is dead, and all subsequent action on that pitch is cancelled.

e. NO PLAYER, MANAGER, OR COACH SHALL CALL TIME, EMPLOY ANY OTHER WORD OR PHRASE, OR COMMIT ANY ACT WHILE THE BALL IS ALIVE AND IN PLAY FOR THE OBVIOUS PURPOSE OF TRYING TO MAKE THE PITCHER COMMIT AN ILLEGAL PITCH.

EFFECT — Sec. 10e: "NO PITCH" shall be declared. The ball is dead, and all subsequent action on that pitch is cancelled. A warning shall be issued to the offending team, and a repeat of this type act by any member of the team warned shall result in the offender being removed from the game.

PLAY — Pitcher is in his windup when the batter, in an attempt to have the pitcher commit an illegal pitch, raises his hand as if to request time. Pitcher stops his windup. RULING — "No pitch" shall be declared.

Sec. 11. THERE SHALL BE ONLY ONE CHARGED CONFERENCE BETWEEN THE MANAGER OR OTHER TEAM REPRESENTATIVE FROM THE DUGOUT WITH EACH PITCHER IN AN INNING. The second charged conference shall result in the removal of the pitcher from the pitching position for the remainder of the game.

Sec. 12. IF THE BALL SLIPS FROM THE PITCHER'S HAND DURING HIS WINDUP OR DURING THE BACKSWING, A BALL IS DECLARED ON THE BATTER, THE BALL WILL REMAIN IN PLAY, AND THE RUNNERS MAY ADVANCE AT THEIR OWN RISK.

RULE 6. PITCHING REGULATIONS (Modified)

Sec. 1. PRELIMINARIES. Before starting the delivery (pitch), the pitcher shall comply with the following:

a. He shall take a position with both feet on the ground and in contact with the pitcher's plate. Both feet must be within the 24-inch length of the pitcher's plate. His shoulders shall be in line with first and third bases. The hands shall be separated. The ball may be in the glove or the pitching hand.
b. While in the position described in *a* above, he shall take the signal from the catcher.
c. After completing *b* above, he shall hold the ball in both hands for not less than 1 second and not more than 10 seconds before releasing it.

PLAY — Pitcher takes a signal while standing within 8 feet of the pitcher's plate but not on the plate. He then assumes legal pitching position for 1 second and pitches the ball. RULING — Illegal pitch. The pitcher must take the signal while legally in contact with the pitcher's plate.

d. The pitcher shall not be considered in pitching position unless the catcher is in position to receive the pitch.
e. The pitcher may not take the pitching position on or near the pitcher's plate without having the ball in his possession.

NOTE: To indicate to the pitcher that he may not start the pitch, the umpire should raise one hand with the palm facing the pitcher. "NO PITCH" shall be declared if the pitcher pitches while the umpire has his hand in said position.

Sec. 2. THE PITCH starts when one hand is taken off the ball or the pitcher makes any motion that is part of his windup.

a. In the act of delivering the ball, the pitcher shall not take more than one step, which must be forward, toward the batter, and simultaneous with the delivery of the ball to the batter. (*Toward the batter* is interpreted as being within the 24-inch length of the pitcher's plate.)

PLAY (1) — The pitcher stands on the right side of the pitcher's plate with both feet in legal contact. He takes a step with his non-pivot foot toward third base so that the entire foot lands to the right and outside of the pitcher's plate. RULING — Illegal Pitch.

b. Pushing off with the pivot foot from a place other than the pitcher's plate is illegal.

NOTE: It is not a step if the pitcher slides his foot across the pitcher's plate, provided contact is maintained with the plate.

Sec. 3. A LEGAL DELIVERY SHALL BE A BALL WHICH IS DELIVERED TO THE BATTER WITH AN UNDERHANDED MOTION.

a. The release of the ball must be on the first forward swing of the pitching arm past the hip. The release must have a complete, smooth follow-through with no abrupt stop of the arm near the hip.
b. The ball must not be outside the pitcher's wrist at the top of the backswing and during the complete forward delivery.
c. On the forward swing of the pitching arm, the elbow must be locked at the point of release, and the driving hip must be squared to home plate when the ball is released.
d. He may take the ball behind the back on the backswing.
e. The pitcher's palm may be pointing downward upon delivery.
f. The pitch is completed with a step toward the batter.
g. The catcher must remain within the lines of the catcher's box until the pitch is released.

PLAY — A pitch is delivered with the catcher outside the boundaries of the catcher's box. RULING — Illegal Pitch.

h. The catcher shall return the ball directly to the pitcher after each pitch, except after a strikeout or a putout made by the catcher.

EXCEPTION: Sec. 3h does not apply when (a) a batter becomes a batter-runner, (b) there are runners on base, or (c) a foul ball is fielded close to the foul line by the catcher who throws to any base for a possible out.

PLAY — Bases are empty, and the batter has a count of no balls and one strike. On the next pitch the batter hits a foul ball which the catcher retrieves and throws to the third baseman. RULING — A ball is awarded to the batter, and the count becomes one ball and two strikes.

i. The pitcher has twenty (20) seconds to release the next pitch after receiving the ball, or after the umpire indicates "play ball."

Sec. 4. THE PITCHER MAY USE ANY WINDUP DESIRED, PROVIDED:

a. He does not make any motion to pitch without immediately delivering the ball to the batter.
b. He does not use a rocker action in which, after having the ball in both hands in the pitch ing position, he removes one hand from the ball, takes a backward and forward swing, and returns the ball to both hands in front of the body.
c. He does not use a windup in which there is a stop or reversal of the forward motion.
d. He does not use a windmill or slingshot-type pitch, or make a complete revolution in the delivery.

NOTE: A *slingshot-type pitch* defined as "turning the body toward first or third base, and bending the elbow during the backswing."

e. He does not continue to wind up after taking the forward step, which is simultaneous with the release of the ball.

Sec. 5. WHILE IN THE PITCHING POSITION, THE PITCHER SHALL NOT DELIBERATELY DROP, ROLL, OR BOUNCE THE BALL IN ORDER TO PREVENT THE BATTER FROM STRIKING IT. A pitchout for the purpose of intentionally walking a batter is not considered an illegal pitch. (Refer to note following Rule 8, Sec. 2c.)

Sec. 6. THE PITCHER SHALL NOT, AT ANY TIME DURING THE GAME, BE ALLOWED TO USE TAPE OR ANY OTHER FOREIGN SUBSTANCE(S) UPON THE BALL, THE PITCHING HAND, OR THE FINGERS; NOR SHALL ANY OTHER PLAYER APPLY ANY FOREIGN SUBSTANCE(S) TO THE BALL. Under the supervision and control of the umpire, powdered resin may be used to dry the hands. The pitcher shall not wear a sweatband, bracelet, or similar-type item on the wrist or forearm of the pitching arm.

Sec. 7. THE PITCHER SHALL NOT DELIVER A PITCH unless all defensive players, except the catcher who must be in the catcher's box, are positioned in fair territory.

NOTE: It is an illegal pitch if a fielder takes a position in the batter's line of vision or, with deliberate unsportsmanlike intent, acts in a manner to distract the batter. A pitch does not have to be released. PENALTY: The offending player shall be ejected from the game, and an illegal pitch shall be declared.

EFFECT — Secs. 1-7: Any infraction of Secs. 1-7 is an illegal pitch, with the exception of Sec. 3f which is covered separately. The ball is dead. A ball is called on the batter. Baserunners are entitled to advance one base without liability to be put out. NOTE: If an illegal pitch hits the batter, the batter is awarded first base and all runners are awarded one base.

EXCEPTION: If the pitcher completes the delivery of the ball to the batter; and if the batter hits the ball and reaches first base safely; and if all baserunners advance at least one base on the action resulting from the batted ball; the play stands, and the illegal pitch is nullified.

NOTE: An illegal pitch shall be called immediately when it becomes illegal. If called by the plate umpire, it shall be called in a voice so that the catcher and the batter will hear it. The plate umpire will also give the delayed dead ball signal. If called by the base umpire, it shall be called so that the nearest fielder shall hear it. The base umpire shall also give the delayed dead ball signal. Failure of players to hear the call shall not void it.

Sec. 8. AT THE BEGINNING OF EACH HALF INNING, OR WHEN A PITCHER RELIEVES ANOTHER, NOT MORE THAN 1 MINUTE MAY BE USED TO DELIVER NOT MORE THAN 3 PITCHES TO THE CATCHER OR OTHER TEAMMATE. Play shall be suspended during this time. For excessive warm-up pitches, a pitcher shall be penalized by awarding a ball to the batter for each pitch in excess of 3.

PLAY — S1 replaces F1. How many throws are permitted for his warm-up? RULING — Three. The umpire is authorized to allow more throws when the weather is inclement or when F1 was removed because of an injury and S1 did not have time to warm up before entering. If F1 returns to pitch in the same inning, no additional warm-up pitches are allowed.

Sec. 9. THE PITCHER SHALL NOT THROW TO A BASE DURING A LIVE BALL WHILE HIS FOOT IS IN CONTACT WITH THE PITCHER'S PLATE AFTER HE HAS TAKEN THE PITCHING POSITION.

EFFECT — Sec. 9: Illegal pitch, the ball is dead, a ball is called on the batter, and all runners are awarded one base. If the throw from the pitcher's plate occurs during a live ball appeal play, the appeal is cancelled.

NOTE: The pitcher may remove himself from the pitching position by stepping backwards off the pitcher's plate. Stepping forward or sideways constitutes an illegal pitch.

Sec. 10. NO PITCH SHALL BE DECLARED WHEN:

a. The pitcher pitches during the suspension of play.
b. The pitcher attempts a quick return of the ball before the batter has taken his position or when the batter is off balance as a result of a previous pitch.
c. A runner is called out for leaving a base prior to the pitcher releasing the pitch.
d. The pitcher pitches before a baserunner has retouched his base after a foul ball has been declared and the ball is dead.

EFFECT — Sec. 10a-d: The ball is dead, and all subsequent action on that pitch is cancelled.

e. NO PLAYER, MANAGER, OR COACH SHALL CALL TIME, EMPLOY ANY OTHER WORD OR PHRASE, OR COMMIT ANY ACT WHILE THE BALL IS ALIVE AND IN PLAY FOR THE OBVIOUS PURPOSE OF TRYING TO MAKE THE PITCHER COMMIT AN ILLEGAL PITCH.

EFFECT — Sec. 10e: "NO PITCH" shall be declared. The ball is dead, and all subsequent action on that pitch is cancelled. A warning shall be issued to the offending team, and repeat of this type act by any member of the team warned shall result in the offender being removed from the game.

PLAY — Pitcher is in his windup when the batter, in an attempt to have the pitcher commit an illegal pitch, raises his hand as if to request time. Pitcher stops his wind up. RULING — "NO PITCH" shall be declared.

Sec. 11. THERE SHALL BE ONLY ONE CHARGED CONFERENCE BETWEEN THE MANAGER OR OTHER TEAM REPRESENTATIVE FROM THE DUGOUT WITH EACH PITCHER IN AN INNING. The second charged conference shall result in the removal of the pitcher from the pitching position for the remainder of the game.

Sec. 12. IF THE BALL SLIPS FROM THE PITCHER'S HAND DURING HIS WIND UP OR DURING THE BACKSWING, A BALL IS DECLARED ON THE BATTER, THE BALL WILL REMAIN IN PLAY, AND THE RUNNERS MAY ADVANCE AT THEIR OWN RISK.

RULE 6. PITCHING REGULATIONS (Slow Pitch)

Sec. 1. THE PITCHER SHALL TAKE A POSITION WITH BOTH FEET FIRMLY ON THE GROUND AND WITH ONE OR BOTH FEET IN CONTACT WITH THE PITCHER'S PLATE. THE PITCHER'S PIVOT FOOT MUST BE IN CONTACT WITH THE PITCHER'S PLATE THROUGHOUT THE DELIVERY.

a. Preliminary to pitching, the pitcher must come to a full and complete stop with the ball in front of the body. The front of the body must face the batter.
b. This position must be maintained at least one (1) second before starting the delivery.
c. The pitcher shall not be considered in pitching position unless the catcher is in position to receive the pitch.

NOTE: To indicate to the pitcher that he may not start the pitch, the umpire should raise one hand with the palm facing the pitcher. "NO PITCH" shall be declared if the pitcher pitches while the umpire has his hand in said position.

Sec. 2. THE PITCH starts when the pitcher makes any motion that is part of his windup after the required pause. Prior to the required pause, any windup may be used. The pivot foot must remain in contact with the pitcher's plate until the pitched ball leaves the hand. If a step is taken, it can be forward or backward, provided the pivot foot is in contact with the pitcher's plate and the step is simultaneous with the release of the ball.

PLAY — F1 has both feet on the pitching plate. He removes one foot by stepping backward and simultaneously pitches ball to B1. B1 does not swing at the pitch. RULING — Legal pitch. A step with the free foot is not required in slow pitch, but if one is taken, it can be forward or backward as long as the pivot foot remains in contact with the pitching plate until the ball is released.

Sec. 3. A LEGAL DELIVERY SHALL BE A BALL WHICH IS DELIVERED TO THE BATTER WITH AN UNDERHANDED MOTION.

PLAY (1) — The pitcher comes to a 2-second stop, takes the ball in his pitching hand over the top of his head, comes down and around in a windmill-type action, and releases the ball the first time past the hip. RULING — Legal. A windmill delivery is legal if the ball is released the first time past the hip and all other aspects of the pitching rule are followed.

PLAY (2) — The pitcher releases the ball during a pitch with his palm on top of the ball and with the ball facing the ground. RULING — Legal.

a. The pitch shall be released at a moderate speed. The speed is left entirely up to the judgement of the umpire. The umpire shall warn the pitcher who delivers a pitch with excessive speed. If the pitcher repeats such an act after being warned, he shall be removed from the pitcher's position for the remainder of the game.

PLAY — After one warning, F1 again delivers a pitch with excessive speed. Plate umpire orders that F1 must be removed from the game. Manager attempts to change F1 to an outfield position, but umpire rules that the pitcher cannot participate in any position for the remainder of the game. RULING — Illegal. F1 shall be removed from the pitching position for the remainder of the game but may participate in the game in any other position.

b. The hand shall be below the hip.
c. The ball must be delivered with a perceptible arc and reach a height of at least 6 feet (1.83 m) from the ground, while not exceeding a maximum height of 12 feet (3.66 m) from the ground.

PLAY — Pitcher releases ball on a pitch to the batter, and it reaches a height of 15 feet before beginning its downward flight toward the plate. RULING — Illegal Pitch.

d. The catcher must remain within the lines of the catcher's box until the pitched ball is batted, touches the ground or plate, or reaches the catcher's box.
e. The catcher shall return the ball directly to the pitcher after each pitch, except after a strikeout, putout made by the catcher, or an attempt by the catcher to throw a runner out at any base after fielding a foul ball close to the foul line.

PLAY — R1 on first base. Count on batter is no balls and one strike. Batter hits a foul ball which the catcher retrieves and gives to the umpire. The umpire gives the catcher a new ball which he throws to the first baseman. RULING — A ball is awarded to the batter. In slow pitch the rule applies regardless of whether or not runners are on base.

f. The pitcher has ten (10) seconds to release the next pitch after receiving the ball, or after the umpire indicates 'play ball'.

EFFECT — Sec. 3e and f: An additional ball is awarded to the batter.

Sec. 4. THE PITCHER MAY USE ANY WINDUP DESIRED, PROVIDED:

a. He does not make any motion to pitch without immediately delivering the ball to the batter.

b. His windup is a continuous motion.

c. He does not use a windup in which there is a stop or reversal of the pitching motion.

d. He delivers the ball toward home plate on the first forward swing of the pitching arm past the hip.

e. He does not continue to wind up after he releases the ball.

f. He does not pitch the ball behind his back or between his legs.

Sec. 5. THE PITCHER SHALL NOT, AT ANY TIME DURING THE GAME, BE ALLOWED TO USE ANY FOREIGN SUBSTANCE(S) UPON THE BALL, THE PITCHING HAND, OR THE FINGERS; NOR SHALL ANY OTHER PLAYER APPLY ANY FOREIGN SUBSTANCE(S) TO THE BALL. Under the supervision and control of the umpire, powdered resin may be used to dry the hands. The pitcher shall not wear a bracelet or similar-type item on the wrist or forearm of the pitching arm.

PLAY (1) — Pitcher with tape on pitching hand. RULING — Legal. Slow pitch pitchers may wear sweat bands on the pitching arm and have tape on the hand or fingers of the pitching hand.

PLAY (2) — The pitcher, holding the ball in his glove hand, delivers the pitch from the glove hand. RULING — Illegal pitch. He must deliver the ball with his bare hand.

Sec. 6. AT THE BEGINNING OF EACH HALF INNING, OR WHEN A PITCHER RELIEVES ANOTHER, NOT MORE THAN 1 MINUTE MAY BE USED TO DELIVER NOT MORE THAN THREE PITCHES TO THE CATCHER OR OTHER TEAMMATE. Play shall be suspended during this time. For excessive warm-up pitches, a pitcher shall be penalized by awarding a ball to the batter for each pitch in excess of three.

Sec. 7. THE PITCHER SHALL NOT ATTEMPT A QUICK RETURN OF THE BALL BEFORE THE BATTER HAS TAKEN HIS POSITION OR WHEN THE BATTER IS OFF BALANCE AS A RESULT OF A PREVIOUS PITCH.

NOTE: It is an illegal pitch if a fielder takes a position in the batter's line of vision or, with deliberate unsportsmanlike intent, acts in a manner to distract the batter. A pitch does not have to be released. PENALTY: The offending player shall be ejected from the game, and an illegal pitch shall be declared.

EFFECT — Secs. 1-7: Any infraction of Secs. 1-7 is an illegal pitch. A ball shall be called on the batter. Baserunners are not advanced.

EXCEPTION: If a batter swings at any illegal pitch, it shall be a strike if missed, foul tipped, or fouled without being caught, and there shall be no penalty for such an illegal pitch. The ball shall remain in play if hit by the batter. If an illegal pitch is called during an appeal play, the appeal is cancelled.

NOTE: An illegal pitch shall be called immediately when it becomes illegal. If called by the plate umpire, it shall be called in a voice so that the catcher and the batter will hear it. The plate umpire will also give the delayed dead ball signal. If called by the base umpire, it shall be called so that the nearest fielder shall hear it. The base umpire shall also give the delayed dead ball signal. Failure of players to hear the call shall not void it.

Sec. 8. NO PITCH SHALL BE DECLARED WHEN:

a. The pitcher pitches during the suspension of play.

b. A runner is called out for leaving his base before the pitched ball reaches home plate or is batted.

c. The pitcher pitches before a baserunner has retouched his base after a foul ball has been declared and the ball is dead.

d. THE BALL SLIPS FROM THE PITCHER'S HAND DURING HIS WINDUP OR DURING THE BACKSWING.

EFFECT — Sec. 8a-d: The ball is dead, and all subsequent action on that pitch is cancelled.

e. NO PLAYER, MANAGER, OR COACH SHALL CALL TIME, EMPLOY ANY OTHER WORD OR PHRASE, OR COMMIT ANY ACT WHILE THE BALL IS ALIVE AND IN PLAY FOR THE OBVIOUS PURPOSE OF TRYING TO MAKE THE PITCHER COMMIT AN ILLEGAL PITCH.

EFFECT — Sec. 8e: "NO PITCH" shall be declared. The ball is dead, and all subsequent action on that pitch is cancelled. A warning shall be issued to the offending team, and a repeat of this type act by any member of the team warned shall result in the offender being removed from the game.

PLAY — Refer to the play following Rule 6, Sec. 10e Effect (Fast Pitch).

Sec. 9. THERE SHALL BE ONLY ONE CHARGED CONFERENCE BETWEEN THE MANAGER OR OTHER TEAM REPRESENTATIVE FROM THE DUGOUT WITH EACH PITCHER IN AN INNING. The second charged conference shall result in the removal of the pitcher from the pitching position for the remainder of the game.

RULE 6. PITCHING (16-Inch Slow Pitch)

Sec. 1. THE PITCHER SHALL TAKE A POSITION WITH BOTH FEET FIRMLY ON THE GROUND AND WITH ONE OR BOTH FEET IN CONTACT WITH THE PITCHER'S PLATE.

a. Preliminary to pitching, the pitcher must come to a full and complete stop with the ball in front of the body.

b. This position must be maintained at least one (1) second before starting the delivery.

c. The pitcher shall not be considered in pitching position unless the catcher is in position to receive the pitch.

NOTE: To indicate to the pitcher that he may not start the pitch, the umpire should raise one hand with the palm facing the pitcher. "NO PITCH" shall be declared if the pitcher pitches while the umpire has his hand in said position.

d. While the pitcher is in the pitching position, in the motion for his delivery, or in the act of faking a delivery prior to a hesitation, the pivot foot must be in contact with the pitcher's plate. After a hesitation, the foot may leave the pitcher's plate during an attempted pickoff or a fake throw. When the pitching motion is restarted, the restriction takes effect again.

Sec. 2. THE PITCH starts when the pitcher makes any motion that is part of his windup after the required pause. Prior to the required pause, any windup may be used. The pivot foot must remain in contact with the pitcher's plate until the pitched ball leaves the hand. If a step is taken, it can be forward or backward, provided the pivot foot is in contact with the pitcher's plate and the step simultaneous with the release of the ball.

PLAY — F1 has both feet on the pitching plate. He removes one foot by stepping backward and simultaneously pitches the ball to B1 who does not swing at the pitch. RULING — Legal pitch. A step with the free foot is not required in slow pitch, but if one is taken, it may be forward or backward as long as the pivot foot remains in contact with the pitching plate until the ball is released.

Sec. 3. A LEGAL DELIVERY SHALL BE A BALL WHICH IS DELIVERED TO THE BATTER WITH AN UNDERHANDED MOTION.

a. The pitch shall be released at a moderate speed. The speed is left entirely up to the judgement of the umpire. The umpire shall warn the pitcher who delivers a pitch with excessive speed. If the pitcher repeats such an act after being warned, he shall be removed from the pitcher's position for the remainder of the game.

b. The hand shall be below the hip.

c. The ball must be delivered with a perceptible arc and reach a height of at least six (6) feet (1.83 m) from the ground while not exceeding a maximum height of twelve (12) feet (3.66 m) from the ground.

d. The catcher must remain within the lines of the catcher's box until the pitched ball is batted, touches the ground or plate, or reaches the catcher's box.

e. The catcher shall return the ball directly to the pitcher after each pitch except after a strikeout or putout made by the catcher.

EXCEPTION: 3e does not apply when the batter becomes a batter-runner or there are baserunners.

PLAY — With R1 on third base, the catcher throws to F5 to pick off the runner after the pitch. The runner is tagged before he returns to the base. RULING — The runner is out.

f. The pitcher has ten (10) seconds to release the next pitch after receiving the ball or after the umpire indicates play ball.

Sec. 4. THE PITCHER MAY USE ANY WINDUP DESIRED, PROVIDING:

a. He does not continue to wind up after he releases the ball.

b. He does not pitch the ball behind his back or between his legs.

c. He does not commit a third hesitation before the mandatory delivery of a pitch, legal or illegal. Hesitations are defined as follows:

(1) Making any motion to pitch without immediately delivering the ball to the batter.

(2) Using a wind up which is not a continuous motion.

(3) Using a wind up in which there is a stop or reversal of the pitching motion.

(4) Not delivering the ball toward home plate on the first forward swing of the pitching arm past the hip.

NOTE: (a) After a hesitation of the pitching motion, and before a restart of that motion, the pitcher may attempt or fake a throw for a pickoff with his pivot foot still in contact with the pitcher's plate.

(b) Runners may be off the bases without penalty during the delivery or fake delivery.

(c) During the pickoff attempt of the pitcher, or the catcher following a pitch, each runner must return to the base at which he was when the pitch was started, and before he is touched with the ball in a fielder's grasp.

(d) If the ball is overthrown, no runners may advance. If the overthrown ball remains in playable territory, the runners are in jeopardy until they return to their original bases.

NOTE: A throw to a base is not considered a hesitation pitch; however a fake to a base is regarded as a hesitation pitch.

PLAY — The pitcher (a) makes one hesitation, throws to 1B to try to pick off the runner, and when the ball is returned, makes another hesitation prior to pitching; (b) makes two hesitations, and as the runner takes off for 2B, either walks off the pitcher's plate toward the runner or steps back off the pitcher's plate and throws to 2B to pick off the runner; (c) throws to 1B to pick off the runner, but the ball is overthrown into the stands; (d) throws to 1B to pick off the runner but the ball is thrown beyond 1B into right field. RULING — (a) Legal; (b) both illegal pitches; (c) the ball is dead, and the runner must return to 1B; (d) the ball remains alive and the runner is in jeopardy until he returns to 1B; no advancement is legal during a pickoff attempt.

Sec. 5. THE PITCHER SHALL NOT, AT ANYTIME DURING THE GAME, BE ALLOWED TO USE ANY FOREIGN SUBSTANCE(S) UPON THE BALL, THE PITCHER'S HAND, OR THE FINGERS; NOR SHALL ANY OTHER PLAYER APPLY ANY FOREIGN SUBSTANCE(S) TO THE BALL. Under the supervision and control of the umpire, powdered resin may be used to dry the hands. The pitcher shall not wear a bracelet or similar-type item on the wrist or forearm of the pitching arm.

PLAY — Pitcher with tape on pitching hand. RULING — Legal. Slow pitch pitchers may wear sweat bands on the pitching arm and have tape on the hand or fingers of the pitching hand.

Sec. 6. AT THE BEGINNING OF EACH HALF INNING, OR WHEN A PITCHER RELIEVES ANOTHER, NOT MORE THAN ONE (1) MINUTE MAY BE USED TO DELIVER NOT MORE THAN THREE (3) PITCHES TO THE CATCHER OR OTHER TEAMMATE. Play shall be suspended during this time. For excessive warm-up pitches, a pitcher shall be penalized by awarding a ball to the batter for each pitch in excess of three (3).

Sec. 7. THE PITCHER SHALL NOT ATTEMPT A QUICK RETURN OF THE BALL BEFORE THE BATTER HAS TAKEN HIS POSITION OR WHEN THE BATTER IS OFF BALANCE AS A RESULT OF A PREVIOUS PITCH.

Sec. 8. A FIELDER SHALL NOT TAKE A POSITION IN THE BATTER'S LINE OF VISION OR, WITH DELIBERATE UNSPORTSMANLIKE INTENT, ACT IN A MANNER TO DISTRACT THE BATTER. A pitch does not have to be released. The offending player shall be ejected from the game.

EFFECT — Secs. 1-8: Any infraction is an illegal pitch. A ball shall be called on the batter, and baserunners may not advance.

EXCEPTION: If a batter swings at any illegal pitch, it shall be a strike if missed, foul tipped, or fouled without being caught, and there shall be no penalty for such an illegal pitch. The ball remains in play if hit by the batter. If an illegal pitch is called during an appeal play, the appeal is cancelled.

NOTE: An illegal pitch shall be called immediately when it becomes illegal. If called by the plate umpire, it shall be called in a voice so that the catcher and the batter will hear it. The plate umpire will also give the delayed dead ball signal. If called by the base umpire, it shall be called so that the nearest fielder shall hear it. The base umpire shall also give the delayed dead ball signal. Failure of players to hear the call shall not void it.

Sec. 9. NO PITCH SHALL BE DECLARED WHEN:

a. The pitcher pitches during the suspension of play.
b. The pitcher pitches before a baserunner has retouched his base after a foul ball has been declared and the ball is dead.
c. The ball slips from the pitcher's hand during his windup or during the backswing.
EFFECT — Secs. 9a-c: The ball is live.
d. No player, manager, or coach shall call time, employ any other word or phrase, or commit any act while the ball is alive and in play for the obvious purpose of trying to make the pitcher commit an illegal pitch.
EFFECT — Sec. 9d: "NO PITCH" shall be declared. The ball is dead, and all subsequent action on that pitch is cancelled. A warning shall be issued to the offending team, and a repeat of this type act by any member of the team warned shall result in the offender being removed from the game.

Sec. 10. THERE SHALL BE ONLY ONE CHARGED CONFERENCE BETWEEN THE MANAGER OR OTHER TEAM REPRESENTATIVE FROM THE DUGOUT WITH EACH PITCHER IN AN INNING. The second charged conference shall result in the removal of the pitcher from the pitching position for the remainder of the game.

RULE 7. BATTING

Sec. 1. THE BATTER SHALL TAKE HIS POSITION WITHIN THE LINES OF THE BATTER'S BOX.

a. The batter shall not have his entire foot touching the ground completely outside the lines of the batter's box, or any part of a foot touching home plate when he hits a ball fair or foul.
b. The batter shall not step directly across in front of the catcher to the other batter's box while the pitcher is in position ready to pitch.
c. The batter shall not enter the batter's box with or use an illegal bat.

PLAY — *Batter hits ball for a single with (a) a bat 35 inches long, or (b) a baseball bat. RULING — In both cases the bats are illegal. The batter-runner is called out, and each runner is returned to the base he occupied at the start of the pitch.*

EFFECT — Sec. 1a-c: The ball is dead, the batter is out, and baserunners may NOT advance.

d. The batter shall not enter the batter's box with or use an altered bat.
EFFECT — Sec. 1d: The ball is dead; the batter is out; and, without warning, he is ejected from the game. Baserunners may not advance.

PLAY — *REFER TO RULE 1, SEC. 1.*

e. The batter must take his position within ten (10) seconds after play ball has been declared by the umpire.
EFFECT — Sec. 1e: If the batter does not enter the batter's box within ten (10) seconds after the umpire calls 'PLAY BALL,' the umpire will call a strike. No pitch has to be thrown. The ball remains dead.

NOTE: This does not pertain to an injured player. If a team has only the required number of players and one cannot participate, the game is forfeited. (See rule 3, section 3g(3) play.)

f. The batter must have both feet completely within the lines of the batter's box prior to the start of the pitch. He may touch the lines, but no part of a foot may be outside the lines prior to the pitch.

NOTE: The umpire should hold up the pitch until the batter is within the lines.

Sec. 2. EACH PLAYER OF THE SIDE AT BAT SHALL BECOME A BATTER IN THE ORDER IN WHICH HIS NAME APPEARS ON THE LINEUP CARD.

a. The batting order of each team must be on the lineup card and must be delivered before the game by the manager or captain to the plate umpire. The plate umpire shall submit it to the inspection of the manager or captain of the opposing team.
b. The batting order delivered to the umpire must be followed throughout the game, unless a player is replaced by a substitute. When this occurs, the substitute must take the place of the removed player in the batting order.
c. The first batter in each inning shall be the batter whose name follows that of the last player who completed a turn at bat in the preceding inning.
EFFECT — Sec. 2b-c: Batting out of order is an appeal play which may be made by the manager, player, or coach of the defensive team only. The defensive team forfeits its right to appeal batting out of order when one legal or illegal pitch has been made to the following batter, or when the pitcher and all infielders have clearly vacated their normal fielding positions and have left fair territory on their way to the bench or dugout area.
NOTE: The offensive team may correct a wrong batter at the plate with no penalty.
(1) If the error is discovered while the incorrect batter is at bat, the correct batter may take his place and legally assume any balls and strikes. Any runs scored or bases run while the incorrect batter was at bat shall be legal.
(2) If the error is discovered after the incorrect batter has completed his turn at bat and before a legal or illegal pitch has been made to the following batter, or before the pitcher and all infielders have clearly vacated their normal fielding positions and have left fair territory on their way to the bench or dugout area,the player who should have batted is out. Any advance or score made because of a ball batted by the improper batter or because of the improper batter's advance to first base as a result of obstruction, an error, a hit batsman, a walk, a dropped third strike, or a basehit shall be nullified. The next batter is the player whose name follows that of the player called out for failing to bat. If the batter declared out under these circumstances is the third out, the correct batter in the next inning shall be the player who would have come to bat had the player been put out by ordinary play.
(3) If the error is discovered after the first legal or illegal pitch to the next batter, or after the pitcher and all infielders have clearly vacated their normal fielding positions and have left fair territory on their way to the bench or dugout area, the turn at bat of the incorrect batter is legal, all runs scored and bases run are legal, and the next batter in order shall be the one whose name follows that of the incorrect batter. No one is called out for failure to bat. Players who have not batted and who have not been called out have lost their turn at bat until reached again in the regular order.
(4) No baserunner shall be removed from the base he is occupying (Except the batter-baserunner who has been taken off the base by the umpire as in (2) above to bat in his proper place). He merely misses his turn at bat with no penalty. The batter following him in the batting order becomes the legal batter.

PLAY — *With R1 on first, B7 is next on the batting list, but B8 erroneously takes his place. The error is discovered by opposing team personnel and reported to the umpire or official scorekeeper (a) after B8 has received two strikes, (b) after B8 has received a base on balls, (c) after B8 has hit a foul which is caught or has made a safe hit to advance R1, (d) after R1 is forced out at 2B and B8 is on first base, (e) after a pitch has been delivered to B9. RULING — In (a) B8 is replaced by B7 who assumes the no ball, two strike count. Any advancement by R1 on first is legal. In (b) and (c) B7 is out. B8 is removed from base and bats again with no balls or strikes. R1 must return to first. In (d) B7 is out, R1 is returned to first, B8 is removed from first, and B8 bats again with no balls and strikes. In (e) no correction is made, and B7 and B8 do not bat again until their regular time.*

d. When the third out in an inning is made before the batter has completed his turn at bat, he shall be the first batter in the next inning, and the ball and strike count on him shall be cancelled.
e. The batting order for co-ed softball shall alternate the sexes. There are no exceptions to this rule.

PLAY (1) — *In a co-ed game, Team A uses six male and four female players for the first three innings. It is detected by the umpire in the fourth inning. RULING: This is a violation of Rule 4, Sec. 6e, and the game is forfeited.*

PLAY (2) — *In a co-ed game, Team B lists a male player, B8, following another male player, B7, in the lineup and the scorebook. Prior to B8 batting his first time, and immediately after B7 bats the first time, the umpire notices the error in the batting order. RULING: Since the actual infraction has not occurred, the umpire should replace B8 with B9 (a female player) and continue the game.*

PLAY (3) — *Team starts the game with six male and six female players, all positioned correctly on defense. After substitutions in the fifth inning, (a) the team plays with six males and four females in the field. No one from either team notices. (b) Two males batted back to back, and after one pitch to the second male batter, the opposing team notifies the umpire of the improper batter. RULING: In (a) there is no penalty. Correct the situation by using the proper number of players and continue to play. In (b) this is considered an illegal re-entry, and the manager as well as the player listed incorrectly on the batting order are ejected from the game.*

PLAY (4) — *In a co-ed game, female #4 bats out of order for female #2 and singles. Male #3 has a count of one ball when the defensive team protests that male #3 is batting out of order. RULING — As soon as one pitch was thrown to male #3, everything female #4 did was legal. Bring male #5 to bat as the proper batter and he will assume the one ball count. Female #2 and male #3 will not bat again until their turn reappears in the batting order.*

Sec. 3. THE BATTER SHALL NOT HINDER THE CATCHER FROM FIELDING OR THROWING THE BALL BY STEPPING OUT OF THE BATTER'S BOX, OR INTENTIONALLY HINDER THE CATCHER WHILE STANDING WITHIN THE BATTER'S BOX.

EFFECT — Sec. 3: The ball is dead, the batter is out, and each baserunner must return to the last base that, in the judgement of the umpire, was touched at the time of the interference.

PLAY — *(FP ONLY) With R1 going to third, B4 steps across home plate to hinder F2 who is fielding the ball or throwing to third. RULING — The batter is declared out. The ball becomes dead immediately, and R1 must return to the base occupied at the time of the pitch.*

Sec. 4. MEMBERS OF THE TEAM AT BAT SHALL NOT INTERFERE WITH A PLAYER ATTEMPTING TO FIELD A FOUL FLY BALL.

EFFECT — Sec. 4: The ball is dead, the batter is out, and each baserunner must return to the base legally held at the time of the pitch.

Sec. 5. THE BATTER SHALL NOT HIT A FAIR BALL WITH THE BAT A SECOND TIME IN FAIR TERRITORY. EXCEPTION: If the batter is standing in the batter's box, a foul ball is ruled even if the ball is hit a second time over fair territory.

NOTE: If the batter drops the bat and the ball rolls against the bat in fair territory, and, in the umpire's judgement, there was no intention to interfere with the course of the ball, the batter is not out, and the ball is alive and in play.

EFFECT — Sec. 5: The ball is dead, the batter is out, and baserunners may not advance.

Sec. 6. A STRIKE IS CALLED BY THE UMPIRE:

a. (FP ONLY) For each legally pitched ball entering the strike zone before touching the ground and at which the batter does not swing.

EFFECT — Sec. 6a: (FP ONLY) The ball is in play, and the baserunners may advance with liability to be put out.

(SP ONLY) For each legally pitched ball entering the strike zone before touching the ground or plate and at which the batter does not swing. It is not a strike if the pitched ball touches home plate and then is swung at by the batter. *Any pitched ball that hits the ground or plate cannot be legally swung at by the batter.* NOTE: If the batter swings and misses the pitch prior to the ball hitting the ground or plate, it is a strike.

EFFECT — Sec. 6a: (SP ONLY) The ball is dead. (EXCEPTION 16'' SP: The ball remains alive, and interference could be involved.)

PLAY — *(16'' SP) Runner on 1B breaks for 2B during the pitch to the plate on a hit and run situation. The pitcher has thrown the pitch short of the plate, and it bounces off the ground towards the catcher. The batter, seeing his runner in trouble, swings at the pitch and basehits into the outfield. The runner from 1B scores, and the batter-runner stops at 2B. RULING: The batter is out for interference, and the runner returns to 1B.*

b. (FP ONLY) For each legally pitched ball struck at and missed by the batter.

EFFECT — Sec. 6b: (FP ONLY) The ball is in play, and the baserunners may advance with liability to be put out.

(SP ONLY) For each pitched ball struck at and missed by the batter.

EFFECT — Sec. 6b: (SP ONLY) The ball is dead.

c. For each foul tip held by the catcher.

EFFECT — Sec. 6c: (FP ONLY) The ball is in play, and baserunners may advance with liability to be put out. The batter is out if it is the third strike.

EFFECT — Sec. 6c: (SP ONLY) The batter is out if it is the third strike. The ball is dead on any strike.

(16-INCH SP ONLY) For each foul tip.

d. (FP ONLY) For each foul ball not legally caught on the fly when the batter has fewer than two strikes.

(SP ONLY) For each foul ball not legally caught, including the third strike.

e. For each pitched ball struck at and missed which touches any part of the batter.

PLAY — *With two strikes, B3 swings at and misses a pitch. Ball strikes his arm or person. RULING — B3 is out.*

f. When any part of the batter's person or clothing is hit with his own batted ball when he is in the batter's box and has fewer than two strikes.

g. When a delivered ball by the pitcher hits the batter while the ball is in the strike zone.

EFFECT — Sec. 6d-g: The ball is dead, and each baserunner must return to his base without liability to be put out.

Sec. 7. A BALL IS CALLED BY THE UMPIRE:

a. (FP ONLY) For each legally pitched ball which does not enter the strike zone, or touches the ground before reaching home plate, or touches home plate, and at which the batter does not swing.

EFFECT — Sec. 7a: (FP ONLY) The ball is in play, and baserunners are entitled to advance with liability to be put out.

(SP ONLY) For each legally pitched ball which does not enter the strike zone, touches the ground before reaching home plate, or touches home plate, and at which the batter does not swing. Any pitched ball that hits the ground or plate cannot be legally swung at by the batter. NOTE: If the batter swings and misses the pitch prior to the ball hitting the ground or plate, it is a strike.

EFFECT — Sec. 7a: (SP ONLY) The ball is dead. Baserunner may not advance. (EXCEPTION 16-INCH SP: The ball remains alive, and interference could be involved.)

PLAY — *The pitcher throws a high arcing pitch which (a) touches ground before reaching the plate, or (b) touches the plate. In each instance the batter swings at the pitch after it hits the ground or plate. RULING: The batter has swung at a dead pitch in each situation. Ignore the strike. Had the batter hit safely, the umpire would nullify the basehit and have him rebat because he has swung at a dead pitch. In each situation a ball is awarded the batter.*

b. (FP ONLY) For each illegally pitched ball not swung at.

EFFECT — Sec. 7b: (FP ONLY) The ball is dead, and baserunners are entitled to advance one base without liability to be put out.

(SP ONLY) For each illegally pitched ball not swung at.

EFFECT — Sec. 7b: (SP ONLY) The ball is dead. Baserunners may not advance. EXCEPTION: If the batter swings at the illegal pitch, the illegal pitch is ignored.

c. (SP ONLY) When a delivered ball by the pitcher hits the batter outside the strike zone.

d. When the catcher fails to return the ball directly to the pitcher as required in Rule 6, Sec. 3e.

e. For each excessive warm-up pitch.

EFFECT — Sec. 7c-e: The ball is dead. Baserunners may not advance.

Sec. 8. A FAIR BALL IS A LEGALLY BATTED BALL WHICH:

a. Settles or is touched on or over fair territory between home and first base or between home and third base.

PLAY — *Batted ball first hits home plate and, without touching any foreign object, settles on fair ground between the pitcher's plate and home plate. RULING — Fair Ball.*

b. Bounds or rolls past first or third base on fair territory.

c. While on or over fair territory, touches the person, attached equipment, or clothing of a player or an umpire.

d. Touches first, second, or third base.

e. First falls or is first touched on or over fair territory beyond first, second, or third base.

EFFECT — Sec. 8a-e: The ball is in play, and baserunners are entitled to advance any number of bases with liability to be put out. The batter becomes a batter-runner unless the infield fly rule applies.

f. While over foul territory, passes out of the playing field beyond the outfield fence.

g. Bounds over any part of the first or third base bag, regardless of where the ball hits after going over the bag.

h. Hits the foul pole above the fence level.

Sec. 9. A FOUL BALL IS A LEGALLY BATTED BALL WHICH:

a. Settles or is touched on or over foul territory between home and first base or between home and third base.

b. Bounds or rolls past first or third base on or over foul territory.

c. While on or over foul territory, touches the person, attached equipment, or clothing of a player or umpire, or any object foreign to the natural ground and provided a fair ball declaration had not been made prior to the ball entering foul territory.

d. First falls or is first touched on or over foul territory beyond first or third base.

e. Touches the batter or the bat in the batter's hands while the ball and the batter are within the batter's box.

f. Immediately rebounds up from the ground or home plate and hits the bat a second time while the batter is in the batter's box.

EFFECT — Sec. 9a-f.

(1) The ball is dead unless it is a legally caught foul fly. If a foul fly is caught, the batter is out.

(2) (FP ONLY) A strike is called on the batter unless he already has two strikes.
(SP ONLY) A strike is called on the batter for each foul ball not legally caught, including the third strike.

(3) Each baserunner must return to his base without liability to be put out, unless a foul fly is caught. In this case baserunners may advance with liability to be put out after the ball has been touched.

Sec. 10. A FOUL TIP IS A BATTED BALL WHICH GOES DIRECTLY FROM THE BAT, NOT HIGHER THAN THE BATTER'S HEAD, TO THE CATCHER'S HAND(S) AND IS LEGALLY CAUGHT BY THE CATCHER.

NOTE: It is not a foul tip unless caught, and any foul tip that is caught is a strike. In fast pitch, modified, and 16-inch slow pitch, the ball is in play. In slow pitch the ball is dead.

PLAY — *A batted ball goes directly to the catcher, hitting his body or equipment no higher than the batter's head, rebounds up in the air and is caught by any fielder. RULING — A dead ball and strike on the batter.*

EFFECT — Sec. 10: (FP ONLY) A strike is called, the ball remains in play, and baserunners may advance with liability to be put out.

EFFECT — Sec. 10: (SP ONLY) A strike is called; the ball is dead.

Sec. 11. THE BATTER IS OUT:

a. When the third strike is struck at, missed, and the ball touches any part of the batter's person.

EFFECT: The ball is dead.

b. When a batter enters the batter's box with, or is discovered using, an altered bat. The batter is also ejected from the game.

c. When the batter enters the batter's box with, or is discovered using, an illegal bat.

PLAY — *REFER TO PLAYS FOLLOWING RULE 1, SECS. 1 AND 31.*

d. When an entire foot is touching the ground completely outside the lines of the batter's box when he hits a ball fair or foul.

e. When any part of a foot is touching home plate when he hits a ball fair or foul.

f. (FP ONLY) When a called or swinging third strike is caught by the catcher.

g. (FP ONLY) When he has three strikes if there are fewer than two outs and first base is occupied. NOTE: Junior Olympic 10-under any time the third strike is dropped.

h. (FP ONLY) When he bunts foul after the second strike. If the ball is caught in the air, it remains alive and in play.

i. (SP ONLY) After a third strike, including an uncaught foul ball that is hit after two strikes.

PLAY — *With a three ball and two strike count, the batter fouls off the next pitch in (a) adult or (b) Junior Olympic play. RULING — The batter is out in both (a) and (b).*

j. (SP ONLY) When he bunts or chops the ball downward.

PLAY — *(SP ONLY) R1 on second. B2 chops down on a pitched ball. F1 throws out R1 advancing to third. RULING — B2 is out for chopping down on the ball. Dead ball. R1 is returned to second.*

Sec. 12. THE BATTER-RUNNER OR BASERUNNER IS NOT OUT IF A FIELDER MAKING A PLAY ON HIM USES AN ILLEGAL GLOVE. The manager of the offended team is given two options:

1) He may have the entire play nullified with each baserunner returning to his original base and the batter-runner batting over and assuming the ball and strike count he had prior to the pitch he hit, or

2) He may take the result of the play and disregard the illegal act.

PLAY — *B1 hits a fly ball to F9. Umpire notices that F9 caught the ball with a first baseman's mitt. RULING — Remove the illegal piece of equipment from the game. Manager of the offended team is given the option of having the entire play nullified with the batter-runner batting over and assuming the ball and strike count he had prior to the pitch he hit, or taking the result of the play and disregarding the illegal catch.*

Sec. 13. ON-DECK BATTER.

a. The on-deck batter is the offensive player whose name follows the name of the batter in the batting order.

b. The on-deck batter shall take a position within the lines of the on-deck circle nearest his bench.

c. The on-deck batter may loosen up with no more than two official softball bats, an approved warm-up bat, or a combination of the two—not to exceed two. Any detachable piece placed on the bat must be approved by the Equipment Standards Committee following a one-year period observed by members of this Committee. NOTE: the "Pow'R Wrap" attachment has been approved beginning with the 1991 season.

d. The on-deck batter may leave the on-deck circle:
(1) When he becomes the batter.
(2) To direct baserunners advancing from third to home plate.

e. When the on-deck batter interferes with the defensive player's opportunity to make an out.

on a runner, the runner closest to home plate at the time of the interference shall be declared out.

f. The provision of Rule 7, Sec. 4, shall apply to the on-deck batter.

RULE 8. BASERUNNING

Sec. 1. THE BASERUNNERS MUST TOUCH BASES IN LEGAL ORDER (I.E., FIRST, SECOND, THIRD, AND HOME PLATE).

a. When a baserunner or batter-runner must return to base(s) while the ball is in play, he must touch the base(s) in reverse order.
EFFECT — Sec. 1a: The ball is in play, and baserunners must return with liability to be put out.

b. When a baserunner or batter-runner acquires the right to a base by touching it before being put out, he is entitled to hold the base until he has legally touched the next base in order, or is forced to vacate it for a succeeding baserunner.

c. When a baserunner dislodges a base from its proper position, neither he nor the succeeding runner(s) in the same series of plays are compelled to follow a base unreasonably out of position.
EFFECT — Sec. 1b-c: The ball is in play, and baserunners may advance with liability to be put out.

d. A baserunner shall not run bases in reverse order either to confuse the fielders or to make a travesty of the game.
EFFECT — Sec. 1d: The ball is dead, and the baserunner is out.

e. Two baserunners may not occupy the same base simultaneously.
EFFECT — Sec. 1e: The runner who first legally occupied the base shall be entitled to it. The other baserunner may be put out by being touched with the ball.

f. Failure of PRECEDING runner to touch a base or to legally tag up on a caught fly ball, and who is declared out, does not affect the status of a SUCCEEDING baserunner who touches bases in proper order; however, if the failure to touch a base in regular order or to legally tag up on a caught fly ball is the third out of the inning, NO SUCCEEDING runner may score a run.

PLAY — REFER TO RULE 5, SEC. 7.

g. No runner may return to touch a missed base or one he had left too soon after a following runner has scored.

h. When the ball becomes dead, no runner may return to touch a missed base or a base left too soon if he has advanced, touched, and remains a base beyond the missed base or the base left to soon. EXCEPTION — Enforce Rule 8, Sec. 5j (2) if the defense intentionally throws the ball out of play to prevent the runner from returning to a base.

i. No runner may return to touch a missed base or one he had left too soon once he enters his team dugout or bench area.

j. When a walk is issued, all runners must touch all bases in legal order. (See Rule 8, Sec. 7f EXCEPTION)

PLAY — In the last of the seventh inning with the score tied, two outs, and bases full, B6 receives a walk to force R1 to home plate. Because B6 assumes that game is over, he fails to go to first and leaves the field. RULING — B6 is out. Run does not count.

k. Bases left too soon on a caught fly ball must be retouched prior to advancing to awarded bases.

l. Awarded bases must also be touched in proper order.

Sec. 2. THE BATTER BECOMES A BATTER-RUNNER:

a. As soon as he hits a fair ball.

b. (FP ONLY) When the catcher fails to catch the third strike before the ball touches the ground when there are fewer than two outs and first base is unoccupied, or anytime there are two outs. This is called the third strike rule. (Exception 10-Under Junior Olympic: The ball is dead and the batter is out.)

PLAY — B1 has two strikes. The next pitch touches the ground in front of home plate and bounces through the strike zone. B1 swings at the pitch, and F2 secures the ball in his mitt after the first bounce. B1 advances to first base while F2 holds the ball. RULING — This is the dropped third strike rule. The batter is not out, and if he beats the throw to first, he is also safe.

EFFECT — Sec. 2a-b: The ball is in play, and the batter becomes a batter-runner with liability to be put out.

c. When four balls have been called by the umpire.
EFFECT — Sec. 2c: (FP ONLY) The ball is in play unless it has been blocked. The batter-runner is entitled to one base without liability to be put out.

NOTE: (FP ONLY) If the pitcher desires to walk a batter intentionally, all defensive players must be stationed anywhere in fair territory, except the catcher who must be in the catcher's box, and the pitcher who must be in a legal pitching position at the start of each pitch. If the defense does not position itself in fair territory, the umpire should call an illegal pitch when the pitch is thrown. See Rule 4, Sec. 2 NOTE and Rule 6, Sec. 7 EFFECT.

EFFECT — Sec. 2c (SP ONLY) The ball is dead. Baserunners may not advance unless forced. If the pitcher desires to walk a batter intentionally, he may do so by notifying the plate umpire who shall award the batter first base. If two batters are to be walked intentionally, the second intentional walk may not be administered until the first batter reaches first base. NOTE: The awards must be made in order, not two at one time.

EFFECT — Sec. 2c: (Co-Ed) The ball is dead. On any walk to a male batter (intentional or not), the next batter — a female — has her choice of walking or hitting up until the first pitch.

NOTE: Should the female batter-runner pass a male batter-runner when choosing to walk, no out shall be called during this dead ball period. A male batter-runner advancing to second without touching first base shall be called out if properly appealed.

d. When the catcher obstructs, or any other fielder interferes with or prevents him from striking at a pitched ball.

EFFECT — Sec. 2d: (1) The umpire shall give a delayed dead ball signal. (2) If the batter hits the ball and reaches first base safely, and if all other runners have advanced at least one base on the batted ball, catcher obstruction is cancelled. All action as a result of the batted ball stands. No option is given. (3) If the manager does not take the result of the play, obstruction is enforced by awarding the batter first base and advancing all other runners only if forced.

PLAY — R1 on first base. The catcher touches the batter's bat prior to or during the swing. Batted ball is grounded to F6 who forces R1 at second base. B2 reaches first base safely. RULING — Since R1 did not advance at least one base, obstruction is called, and the manager of the offensive team is given an option. He may take the result of the play, or he may accept the award for catcher obstruction, in which case R1 would be awarded second base, and B2 would be awarded first base.

e. When a fair batted ball strikes the person, attached equipment, or clothing of an umpire or a baserunner on or over fair or foul ground. If the baserunner is hit with a fair batted ball while touching a base, he is not out.
EFFECT — Sec. 2e: If the ball hits an umpire or baserunner (a) after touching a fielder (including the pitcher) the ball is in play (Rule 8, Sec. 9e); (b) after passing a fielder other than the pitcher, and provided no other infielder had a chance to make an out, the ball is in play (Rule 8, Sec. 9d); or (c) before passing a fielder without being touched, the ball is dead. In (c), if the baserunner is hit by the ball while off base, he is out, and the batter-runner is entitled to first base without liability to be put out. Any baserunner not forced by the batter-runner must return to the base he had reached prior to the interference. When a fair ball touches a baserunner who is in contact with a base, the ball remains dead or alive depending on the position of the fielder closest to the base.

PLAY — With R1 on third and R2 on first, a ball batted by B3 strikes umpire who is: (a) on fair territory behind third baseman, or (b) behind the pitcher but in front of an infielder. RULING — In (a) ball remains alive since it has passed a fielder. In (b), unless ball touches F1, it becomes dead, and each runner is sent to the base he occupied or to which he was being forced when the ball became dead (i.e., R1 remains on third, and R2 and B3 go to second and first respectively).

f. (FP ONLY) When a pitched ball not swung at or not called a strike touches any part of the batter's person or clothing while he is in the batter's box. It does not matter if the ball strikes the ground before hitting him. The batter's hands are not to be considered as part of the bat.
EFFECT — Sec. 2f: The ball is dead, and the batter is entitled to one base without liability to be put out, unless he made no effort to avoid being hit. In this case the plate umpire calls either a ball or a strike.

Sec. 3. BASERUNNERS ARE ENTITLED TO ADVANCE WITH LIABILITY TO BE PUT OUT:

a. (FP ONLY) When the ball leaves the pitcher's hand on his delivery.
b. When the ball is thrown into fair or foul territory and is not blocked.
c. On a fair batted ball that is not blocked.
d. When a legally caught fly ball is first touched.
e. If a fair ball strikes an umpire or a baserunner after having passed an infielder other than the pitcher, and provided no other infielder had a chance to make an out; or when a fair batted ball has been touched by an infielder, including the pitcher. The ball shall be considered in play.
EFFECT — Sec. 3a-e: The ball is alive and in play.

Sec. 4. A PLAYER FORFEITS HIS EXEMPTION FROM LIABILITY TO BE PUT OUT:

a. If, while the ball is in play, he fails to touch the base to which he was entitled before attempting to make the next base. If the runner put out is the batter-runner at first base, or any other baserunner forced to advance because the batter became a batter-runner, this out is a force out.
b. If, after overrunning first base, the batter-runner attempts to continue to second base.
c. If, after dislodging a base, a baserunner tries to continue to the next base.
d. (16-INCH SP ONLY) A player may lead off any base with the risk of being picked off by a throw from the pitcher or catcher. If a throw from the pitcher or catcher results in an overthrown or blocked ball, no runners may advance. Any runner advancing on a pitch not hit is liable to be put out if tagged before returning to his original base.

PLAY — R1 leads off first base and advances to second on the pitch. The ball is thrown by F2 to F4 who tags R1 while R1 is standing on second base. RULING — R1 is out. He may lead off, but he must return to his base before being tagged if the ball is not hit.

Sec. 5. BASERUNNERS ARE ENTITLED TO ADVANCE WITHOUT LIABILITY TO BE PUT OUT:

a. When forced to vacate a base because the batter was awarded a base on balls.
EFFECT — Sec. 5a: (FP ONLY) The ball remains in play unless it is blocked. Any baserunner affected is entitled to one base and may advance farther at his own risk if the ball is in play.
EFFECT — Sec. 5a: (SP ONLY) The ball is dead.
b. When a fielder (1) not in possession of the ball, (2) not in the act of fielding a batted ball, or (3) not about to receive a thrown ball, impedes the progress of a baserunner or batter-runner who is legally running bases.
EFFECT — Sec. 5b: When any obstruction occurs (including a rundown), the umpire will signal a delayed dead ball. The ball will remain alive.
(1) If the obstructed runner is put out prior to reaching the base he would have reached had there not been obstruction, a dead ball is called, and the obstructed runner — and each other runner affected by the obstruction — will always be awarded the base or bases he would have reached, in the umpire's judgement, had there not been obstruction. This baserunner would either be advanced or returned to the last base touched. An obstructed runner may never be called out between the two bases where he was obstructed. Should an act of interference occur following any obstruction, enforcement of the interference penalty would have precedence.
(2) If the obstructed runner is put out after passing the base he would have reached had there not been obstruction, the obstructed runner will be called out. The ball remains alive.

(3) When a runner, while advancing or returning to a base, is obstructed by a fielder who neither has the ball nor is attempting to field a batted or thrown ball, or a fielder who fakes a tag without the ball, the obstructed runner — and each other runner affected by the obstruction — will always be awarded the base or bases he would have reached, in the umpire's judgement, had there been no obstruction. If the umpire feels there is justification, a defensive player making a fake tag could be removed from the game.

NOTE: Obstructed runners are still required to touch all bases in proper order, or they could be called out on a proper appeal by the defensive team.

PLAY (1) —   With R1 on third and R2 on second, R1 is caught between third and home. As R1 is attempting to regain third, F5 obstructs him. RULING — A delayed dead ball is signaled by the umpire. If R1 is tagged out, the ball is dead, obstruction is declared, and R1 awarded third. If the ball is overthrown, R1 and R2 may advance to home. If R1 is awarded third, R2 is returned to second base.

PLAY (2) —   The ball is hit to F9. As R1 passes first base, he is obstructed while no play is being made on him. He is thrown out by a wide margin at home plate. RULING — If, in the judgment of the umpire, R1 advanced beyond the base he would have made had he not been obstructed, he is out.

PLAY (3) —   R1 is on first when B2 hits a ball between the right and center fielders. In rounding second base, R1 falls after colliding with the shortstop, gets up and continues toward home plate. The relay throw from the second baseman to the catcher arrives when R1 is about five feet from the plate. R1 crashes into the fielder who is holding the ball. Because of the collision, the ball is dropped, and R1 scores. Should the umpire call R1 out? RULING: Yes. If R1 had not crashed into the catcher, he probably would have been awarded home due to the obstruction by the shortstop, however, because of the deliberate crash (interference), the obstruction is ignored and the runner will be called out under Rule 8, Section 8s.

(4) Catcher obstruction is covered under Rule 8, Sec. 2d.

c. (FP ONLY) When a wild pitch or passed ball lodges in or goes under, over, or through the backstop.
EFFECT — Sec. 5c: The ball is dead. All baserunners are awarded one base only. The batter is awarded first base only on the fourth ball.

d. When forced to vacate a base because the batter was awarded first base.
(1) (FP ONLY) For being hit by a pitched ball.
(2) For being obstructed by the catcher when striking at a pitched ball.
EFFECT — Sec. 5d (1)-(2): The ball is dead, and each baserunner may not advance farther than the base to which he is entitled.
(3) (FP ONLY) If, with a runner on third base trying to score by means of a squeeze play or a steal, the catcher or any other fielder steps on or in front of home plate without possession of the ball, or touches the batter or his bat, the pitcher shall be charged with an illegal pitch, the batter shall be awarded first base on the obstruction, each other runner shall be awarded one base on the illegal pitch, and the ball is dead.

PLAY —   R1 is on third base. A squeeze play is in progress, but as the batter attempts to bunt the pitched ball, he is obstructed by the catcher. RULING — Illegal pitch, and obstruction is declared. R1 is awarded home plate, and batter is awarded first base.

e. (FP ONLY) When a pitcher makes an illegal pitch.
EFFECT — Sec. 5e: The ball is dead, and each baserunner may advance to the base to which he is entitled without liability to be put out.

f. When a fielder contacts or catches a fair batted or thrown ball with his cap, helmet, mask, protector, pocket, detached glove, or any part of his uniform which is detached from its proper place on his person.
EFFECT — Sec. 5f: The baserunners would be entitled to three bases from the time of the pitch if a batted ball, or two bases from the time of the throw if a thrown ball, and in either case, they may advance farther at their own risk. If the illegal catch or touch is made on a fair hit ball which, in the judgement of the umpire, would have cleared the outfield fence in flight, the batter-runner shall be awarded a home run.

PLAY —   R1 is on second and R2 is on first when B3 hits ground ball to F6. F6 fields the ball, steps on second for a force on R2 advancing from first, and then throws wildly to F3. F3 tosses his mitt into the air striking the ball. The ball bounces into the dugout. RULING — R2 is out. Both R1 and B3 are awarded two bases each from their positions at the time the ball left the fielder's hand. On this play the award for detached equipment and for an overthrown ball going out of play, are the same.

g. When the ball is in play and is overthrown (beyond the boundary lines) or is blocked.
EFFECT — Sec. 5g. All runners will be awarded two bases, and the award will be governed by the positions of the runners when the ball left any fielder's hand. If two runners are between the same bases, the award is based on the position of the lead runner.
EXCEPTION: (1) When a fielder loses possession of the ball, such as on an attempted tag, and the ball enters the dead ball area or becomes blocked, each runner is awarded one base from the last base touched at the time the ball entered the dead ball area or became blocked. (2) If a runner touches the next base and returns to his original base, the original base he left is considered the ''last base touched'' for the purpose of an overthrow award.

PLAY (1) —   R1 and R2 are on second and first bases respectively. B3 hits the ball to F6 who muffs it, recovers it, and then throws late to F3 in an attempt to retire B3. R1 and R2 reach third and second bases respectively. R1 attempts to advance to home, thereby drawing a throw from F3 which goes into the dugout. RULING — R1 and R2 are awarded home, and B3 is awarded third.

PLAY (2) —   R1 on first. B2 hits ground ball to F6. F6 flips the ball to F4 for force out on R1. Relay to F3 from F4 goes into the dugout area. B2 had already passed first base before relay was made. RULING — B2 is awarded third base. Award of bases is governed by the position of each runner and the last base he has touched at the time of the throw.

PLAY (3) —   No runners on base. B1 hits ball to F10 who throws it to F3 to force out B1. B1 is already past first base when ball is released by F10. The ball bounces past F3 and into the stands. RULING — B1 is awarded third base.

PLAY (4) —   A thrown ball hits a bat or glove lying on the ground (other than the bat discarded by the batter). RULING — (1) If the bat or glove belongs to the team at bat, it is ruled interference, and the player being played on shall be declared out. The ball is dead, and all baserunners must return to the last base touched prior to the thrown ball hitting the bat or glove. (2) If the bat or glove belongs to the team in the field, it becomes a blocked ball, and the overthrow rule applies. (3) If no apparent play is obvious, no one is called out, but each runner must return to the last base touched at the time the ball hit the illegal equipment of the offensive team.

h. When a fair batted fly ball strikes the foul pole above fence level or leaves the playing field in fair territory without touching the ground or going through the fence. It shall entitle the batter-runner to a home run, unless it passes out of the grounds at a distance less than the prescribed fence distances from home plate (as outlined in Rule 2, Sec. 1), in which case the batter-runner would be entitled to only two bases. The batter-runner must touch the bases in regular order. The point at which the stands or fence is less than the distance listed (Rule 2, Sec. 1) from home plate shall be clearly marked for the umpire's information.
EXCEPTION: See the note after Rule 5, Sec. 9)

PLAY —   A fair batted ball touches (a) F9's glove and goes over the fence in fair territory, (b) F9's glove and goes over the fence in foul territory, (c) the top of a fence railing and goes over, (d) the top of a fence railing, bounds to F9's glove, and then goes over the fence in fair territory. RULING — A home run in (c), and a two-base hit in (b). In both (a) and (d), it is a home run in fast pitch and a four-base award in slow pitch.

i. When a fair ball bounds or rolls over, under, or through a fence; bounds over, under or through any obstruction marking the boundaries of the playing field; is unintentionally caused to go out of play when it bounds off a defensive player; or is unintentionally caused to go out of play when it bounds off a baserunner or an umpire after having touched or been touched by a defensive player, or after having passed an infielder, excluding the pitcher, and provided no other infielder had a chance to make an out.
EFFECT — Sec. 5i: The ball is dead, and all baserunners are awarded two bases from the time of the pitch.

j. (1) When a live ball is unintentionally carried by a fielder from playable territory into dead ball territory, the ball becomes dead. Each baserunner is awarded one base from the last base touched at the time fielder enters dead ball territory.

NOTE: A fielder carrying a live ball into the dugout or team area to tag a player is considered to have unintentionally carried it there.

(2) If, in the judgement of the umpire, a fielder intentionally carries, kicks, pushes, or throws a live ball from playable territory into dead ball territory, the ball becomes dead, and each baserunner is awarded two bases from the last base touched at the time the fielder entered or the ball was kicked, pushed, or thrown into dead ball territory.

NOTE: A dead ball line is considered in play.

Sec. 6. A BASERUNNER MUST RETURN TO HIS BASE:

a. When a foul ball is illegally caught and so declared by the umpire.
b. When an illegally batted ball is declared by the umpire.
c. When a batter, batter-runner, or baserunner is called out for interference. Each other baserunner shall return to the last base which was, in the judgement of the umpire, legally touched by him at the time of the interference.
d. (FP ONLY) When the plate umpire or his clothing interferes with the catcher's attempt to throw.

PLAY —   With R1 attempting to steal, umpire interferes with catcher's throw. RULING — Umpire signals delayed dead ball. If R1 is not put out, umpire declares a dead ball, and R1 must return to the base he occupied before the interference.

e. When any part of the batter's person or clothing is touched by a pitched ball that is swung at and missed.
f. (FP ONLY) When a batter is hit by a pitched ball, unless forced.
g. When a foul ball is not caught.
EFFECT — Sec. 6a-g:
(1) The ball is dead.
(2) Each baserunner must return to his base without liability to be put out, except when forced to go to the next base because the batter became a batter-runner.
(3) No runs shall score unless all bases are occupied.
(4) Baserunners need not touch the intervening bases in returning to base, but must return promptly; however, they must be allowed sufficient time to return.

h. (SP ONLY) Base stealing is not allowed.
EFFECT — Sec. 6h: Each baserunner may leave his base when a pitched ball is batted, touches the ground, or reaches home plate, but must return to that base immediately after each pitch not hit by the batter. (16-INCH SP ONLY) Baserunners may lead off prior to a pitched ball.

i. When a caught fair fly ball, including a line drive (FP and SP) or bunt (FP ONLY), which can be caught by an infielder with ordinary effort, is intentionally dropped with fewer than two outs and a runner on first base; first and second; first and third; or first, second, and third bases.

PLAY —   REFER TO RULE 7, SEC. 11h EFFECT.

j. (10-Under Junior Olympic Fast Pitch ONLY) Under no condition is a runner permitted to steal a base when a pitched ball is not batted. Each baserunner may leave his base when the ball leaves the pitcher's hand, but the ball is dead if not hit, and he must return to his base without liability to be put out.

Sec. 7. BATTER-RUNNER IS OUT:

a. (FP ONLY) When the catcher drops the third strike and he is legally touched with the ball by a fielder before touching first base.
b. (FP ONLY) When the catcher drops the third strike and the ball is held on first base before the batter-runner reaches it.

c. When, after a fair ball is hit, he is legally touched with the ball before he touches first base.

d. When, after a fair ball is hit, the ball is held by a fielder touching first base with the ball or any part of his person before the batter-runner touches first base.

PLAY — *The first baseman has the ball in his right hand while lying on the ground. He touches first base with his left hand prior to the batter-runner reaching first base. RULING — The batter-runner is out.*

e. When, after a fly ball is hit, the ball is caught by a fielder before it touches the ground or any object or person other than a defensive player.

EFFECT — Sec. 7a-e: The ball is in play, and the batter-runner is out.

f. When he fails to advance to first base and enters his team area after a batted fair ball, a base on balls, a hit batsman (FP ONLY), a dropped third strike (FP ONLY), or catcher obstruction.

EXCEPTION: In slow pitch, the ball is dead on a base on balls, the batter-runner is out, and runners cannot advance.

PLAY (1) — *Batter hits ground ball to pitcher. Pitcher hesitates in throwing ball to first base. Batter-runner, assuming he is an "easy out," enters his team area (bench, dugout, etc.). Pitcher finally throws to first base, but ball is not caught by first baseman and rolls into the dugout. Batter-runner then leaves his team area and runs to first base. RULING — Batter-runner is out.*

PLAY (2) — *REFER TO RULE 8, SEC. 1j.*

g. When he runs outside the 3-foot (0.91 m) line and, in the judgement of the umpire, interferes with the fielder taking the throw at first base; however, he may run outside the 3-foot (0.91 m) line to avoid a fielder attempting to field a batted ball.

h. When he interferes with a fielder attempting to field a batted ball, interferes with a thrown ball, or (FP ONLY) interferes with a dropped third strike. If this interference, in the judgement of the umpire, is an obvious attempt to prevent a double play, the baserunner closest to home plate shall also be called out. NOTE: A batter-runner or baserunner being hit with a thrown ball does not necessarily constitute interference.

i. When he interferes with a play at home plate in an attempt to prevent an obvious out at home plate. The runner is also out.

PLAY — *No outs. R1 on third base. Batter hits a ground ball to the first baseman and then interferes with first baseman's throw to home plate for a play on R1. RULING — Batter-runner and R1 are both declared out.*

j. When he moves back toward home plate to avoid or delay a tag by a fielder.

k. When he hits a fair batted ball with an altered or illegal bat.

EFFECT — Sec. 7g-k: The ball is dead, and the batter-runner is out. Each other baserunner must return to the last base legally touched at the time of or before the illegal action.

NOTE: In the case of an altered bat, the player is also ejected from the game.

l. Immediately when he hits an infield fly, as declared by the umpire, with runners on first and second or on first, second, and third with fewer than two outs. This is called the IN-FIELD FLY RULE.

PLAY (1) — *Umpire declares an infield fly, but ball curves to foul area. RULING — Announcement is reversed. It is not an infield fly but an ordinary foul. Batter is not out unless foul is caught. If caught, each runner must retouch his base before advancing.*

PLAY (2) — *REFER TO RULE 1, SEC. 40.*

m. If an infielder intentionally drops a fair ball, including a line drive (FP or SP) or a bunt (FP ONLY), which can be caught with ordinary effort with first; first and second; first and third; or first, second, and third bases occupied with fewer than two outs.

NOTE: A trapped ball shall not be considered as having been intentionally dropped.

EFFECT — Sec. 11h: The ball is dead, and each baserunner must return to the last base touched at the time of the pitch.

PLAY — *With one out and R1 on first, B3 hits a fly ball. F4 guides the ball into his hands but intentionally drops it in an attempt to complete a double play. RULING — Umpire should immediately declare B3 out. Ball is dead. Baserunners may not advance.*

n. If the immediate preceding runner who is not yet out intentionally interferes, in the umpire's judgement, with a fielder who is attempting to catch a thrown ball in an attempt to complete the play. Interference shall be declared, and the runner shall also be called out.

o. (SP ONLY) For excess over-the-fence home runs as listed under Rule 5, Section 9.

Sec. 8. THE BASERUNNER IS OUT:

a. When running to any base in regular or reverse order and he runs more than 3 feet (0.91 m) from a direct line between that base and the next one to avoid being touched by the ball in the hand(s) of a fielder.

b. When the ball is in play and while he is not in contact with a base, he is legally touched with the ball in the hand(s) of a fielder.

c. When, on a force play, a fielder contacts the base while holding the ball, touches the ball to the base, or tags the runner before he reaches the base.

d. When he fails to return to touch the base he previously occupied when play is resumed after suspension of play.

e. When he physically passes a preceding baserunner before that runner has been put out.

EFFECT — Sec. 8a-e: The ball is in play, and the baserunner is out.

PLAY — *With R1 on first, B2 hits a double. A throw to third drives R1 back to second. B2 has rounded second and discovers he has passed R1. He runs back and finally reaches first without being tagged out. RULING — B2 is out as soon as he passes R1.*

f. When he leaves his base to advance to another base before a caught fly ball has touched a fielder, provided the ball is returned to an infielder and properly appealed.

PLAY — *No outs. R1 on third base. B2 hits fly ball to F7. F7 misjudges flight of ball, and it hits him on the shoulder, deflects into the air to F8, and is legally caught by F8 before it hits the ground. R1 tags up at third base as soon as ball hits F7*

on the shoulder but before F8 holds ball securely in glove. RULING — Legal advance. Run counts. R1 may leave base as soon as ball is touched.

g. When he fails to touch the intervening base or bases in regular or reverse order and the ball is returned to an infielder and properly appealed.

PLAY (1) — *With R1 on first, B2 hits safely to right field. An overthrow at first: (a) goes into the stands, (b) strikes the enclosing wall and rebounds to the catcher. In going to third base, R1 misses second base. He had passed second or was approaching second when the ball left the hand of F9. The ball is then thrown to second for an appeal. RULING — In (a), if R1 has reached second base by the time the throw leaves the hand of F9, he is awarded home plate. If the appeal is properly made, it should be allowed, and the run scored by R1 is cancelled. If R1 has not reached second by the time the throw leaves the hand of F9, he is awarded third base. A proper appeal should be allowed and enforced. In (b) R1 is out on the appeal since the ball is not blocked, and no bases are awarded.*

PLAY (2) — *REFER TO RULE 1, SEC. 2.*

h. When the batter-runner legally overruns first base, attempts to run to second base, and is legally touched while off base.

PLAY — *B1 reaches first safely, but in his overrun he breaks for second and then "gives up" while far away from the baseline. RULING — If B1 is attempting to reach a base, he must be tagged, but the fielder is not expected to chase him into the outfield. In the outlined case he is out for being out of the baseline.*

i. When running or sliding for home plate and he fails to touch it, makes no attempt to return to it, and a fielder holds the ball in his hand while touching said plate and appeals to the umpire for the decision.

EFFECT — Sec. 8f-i:
(1) These are appeal plays, and the defensive team loses the privilege of putting the baserunner out if the appeal is not made before the next legal or illegal pitch, or before the pitcher and all infielders have clearly vacated their normal fielding positions and have left fair territory on their way to the bench or dugout area.

(2) If properly appealed during a live ball, the baserunner is out. Item (3) below covers dead ball appeals.

NOTE: On appeal plays the appeal must be made before the next legal or illegal pitch, or before the defensive team has left the field. The defensive team has "left the field" when the pitcher and all infielders have clearly vacated their normal fielding positions and have left fair territory on their way to the bench or dugout area.

(3) Once the ball has been returned to the infield and time has been called, any infielder (including the pitcher or catcher), with or without possession of the ball, may make a verbal appeal on a runner missing a base or leaving a base too soon on a caught fly ball. The administering umpire should acknowledge the appeal and then make a decision on the play. No baserunner may leave his base during this period as the ball remains dead until the next pitch.

NOTE: (a) If the pitcher has possession of the ball and is in contact with the pitching plate when making a verbal appeal, no illegal pitch is called. (b) If play ball has been declared by the umpire and the pitcher then requests an appeal, the umpire would again call time and allow the appeal process.

PLAY (1) — *Runner R2 leaves second base too soon on a fly ball caught by F7. The ball is thrown directly into the infield with an appeal made by F4 at second base. RULING: The ball has remained alive, and when the proper appeal is made, R2 is called out.*

PLAY (2) — *Runner R1 on second base and R2 on first base. Batter B3 hits a fly ball to F7. Both runners advance; however, R1 leaves too soon. Time is called. The pitcher has the ball, and after the umpire recognized the appeal, (a) he announces to the umpire that he wants to appeal R1 leaving too soon, (b) he carries the ball over and touches R1 standing on third base, (c) he throws the ball to F4 who touches second base, or (d) he fakes a throw toward third base, and the runner steps off the base. RULING: In all cases the ball is dead, and no baserunner may leave his base. The proper appeal is (a); however, (b) and (c) are acceptable. With the ball dead in (d), there is no penalty for the runner stepping off the base.*

j. When he interferes with a fielder attempting to field a batted ball or interferes with a thrown ball. If this interference, in the judgement of the umpire, is an obvious attempt to prevent a double play and occurs before the baserunner is put out, the immediate succeeding runner shall also be called out.

PLAY — *With R1 on first, B1 hits the ball on the ground between first and second. R1 is struck by the batted ball before it passes a fielder, or he hinders F4 in his throw to first. RULING — R1 is out, and the ball becomes dead when the interference occurs. If the interference clearly prevented B2 from being put out at first, he also is out.*

k. When he is struck with a fair untouched batted ball in fair territory while not in contact with a base and before it passes an infielder, excluding the pitcher.

NOTE: Sec. 8j-k. When baserunners are called out for interference, the batter-runner is awarded first base and credited with a base hit.

PLAY — *R1 is (a) between second and third or (b) touching second. He is struck by B3's untouched batted ball before it passes a fielder, excluding the pitcher. RULING — Ball becomes dead in (a) and (b). R1 is out in (a). He is not out in (b). The batter-runner is entitled to first base in both cases.*

l. When he intentionally kicks a ball which an infielder has missed.

m. When anyone, other than another baserunner, physically assists him while the ball is in play. If this assistance occurs prior to a caught or uncaught batted fly ball, regardless of whether the ball is fair or foul, a delayed dead ball call will be made, after which he will be declared out. If the ball is caught, the batter-runner will also be declared out. (NOTE: The ball is dead if not caught. If a fair ball, award the batter-runner one base, and if a foul ball, the batter will bat again.)

n. When the coach near third base runs in the direction of home plate on or near the baseline while a fielder is attempting to make a play on a batted or thrown ball and thereby draws a throw to home plate. The runner closest to home shall be declared out.

o. When one or more members of the offensive team stand or collect at or around a base to which a baserunner is advancing, thereby confusing the fielders and adding to the difficulty of making the play.

NOTE: Members of a team include bat boy or any other person authorized to sit on team's bench.

p. When he runs the bases in reverse order to confuse the defensive team or to make a travesty of the game. (See Rule 8, Sec. 7j.)

q. If a coach intentionally interferes with a thrown ball while in the coach's box, or interferes with the defensive team's opportunity to make a play on another runner. The runner closest to home plate at the time of the interference shall also be declared out.

r. When, after being declared out, he interferes with a defensive player's opportunity to make a play on another runner. The runner closest to home plate at the time of the interference shall also be declared out.

EFFECT — Sec. 8j-r: The ball is dead, and the baserunner is out. Each other baserunner must return to the last base legally touched at the time of or before the illegal action.

NOTE: When a runner after scoring, interferes with a defensive player, the runner closest to home shall be called out.

PLAY — R1 on third base and R2 on first base. Batter hits a sharp grounder to second baseman who tags R2 out. R2 then interferes with the second baseman's attempt to throw to first to retire the batter-runner. RULING — Ball becomes dead, and R1 is also called out. Batter-runner is awarded first base.

s. When a defensive player has the ball and the runner remains on his feet and deliberately, with great force, crashes into the defensive player.

EFFECT — Sec. 8s: The runner is out, the ball is dead, and each other baserunner must return to the last base touched at the time of the collision, unless Rule 8, Sec. 8j or Rule 8, Sec. 8r applies.

NOTE: If the act is determined to be flagrant, the offender shall be ejected.

PLAY — The catcher has received the ball and is waiting to tag the runner attempting to score. The runner deliberately runs into the catcher with great force, causing him to drop the ball. RULING — The runner is out. He is also ejected if the act is flagrant.

t. (FP ONLY) When he fails to keep contact with the base to which he is entitled until the ball leaves the pitcher's hand. When a baserunner is legitimately off his base after a pitch or as a result of a batter completing his turn at bat, and while the pitcher has the ball within an 8-foot (2.44 m) radius of the pitcher's plate, he must immediately return to his base or attempt to advance to the next base.

(1) Failure to immediately return to his base or proceed to the next base once the pitcher has the ball within the 8-foot (2.44m) radius of the pitcher's plate will result in the baserunner being declared out.

(2) Once the runner returns to a base for any reason, he will be declared out if he leaves said base, unless a play is made on him or another runner (a fake throw is considered a play), the pitcher no longer has possession of the ball within the 8-foot (2.44 m) radius, or the pitcher releases the ball on a pitch to the batter.

NOTE: A base on balls or dropped third strike on which a runner is entitled to run is treated the same as a batted ball. The batter-runner may continue past first base and is entitled to run toward second base as long as he does not stop at first base. If he stops after he rounds first base, he then must comply with Sec. 8t(1).

PLAY — With R1 on second, B2 takes a called third strike for the first out of the inning; meanwhile, R1 leads off second base after delivery to the plate. Catcher returns ball to the pitcher who has it within the 8-foot (2.44 m) radius of the pitcher's plate. The runner at this moment makes no attempt to move either way. RULING — The runner must immediately return to second or immediately advance to the next base. Failure to immediately return to his base or proceed to the next base once the pitcher has the ball within the 8-foot (2.44 m) radius of the pitcher's plate will result in the baserunner being declared out.

u. (SP ONLY) When he fails to keep contact with the base to which he is entitled until a pitched ball touches the ground, reaches home plate, or is batted. EXCEPTION (16-INCH SP ONLY) Any runner may leave his base as soon as the ball is declared in play.

EFFECT — Sec. 8t-u: The ball is dead, "NO PITCH" is declared, and the baserunner is out.

v. When he abandons a base and enters his team area or leaves the field of play. The baserunner shall be declared out immediately when he enters his team area or leaves the field of play.

w. When he positions himself behind and not in contact with a base to get a running start on any fly ball. The ball remains alive.

Sec. 9. BASERUNNER IS NOT OUT:

a. When he runs behind or in front of the fielder and outside the baseline in order to avoid interfering with a fielder attempting to field the ball in the base path.

b. When he does not run in a direct line to a base, provided the fielder in the direct line does not have the ball in his possession.

c. When more than one fielder attempts to field a batted ball and the baserunner comes into contact with the one who, in the judgement of the umpire, was not entitled to field the ball.

d. When he is hit with a fair, untouched batted ball that has passed an infielder, excluding the pitcher, and, in the judgement of the umpire, no other infielder HAD A CHANCE TO MAKE AN OUT.

PLAY (1) — With R1 on second, B2 hits ball behind F6 who is playing in. Batted ball touches R1 and is deflected to foul ground. RULING — If the touching of R1 is accidental, it is ignored because batted ball has passed a fielder. If R1 intentionally deflected batted ball, umpire will rule interference, with ball becoming dead and R1 being declared out.

PLAY (2) — A batted ball strikes third base and then caroms to foul territory where it strikes R1 who is leading off third. RULING — R1 is out, and ball is dead.

e. When he is hit by a fair batted ball after it touches or is touched by any fielder, including the pitcher, and he could not avoid contact with the ball.

f. When he is touched with a ball not securely held by a fielder.

g. When the defensive team does not request the umpire's decision on an appeal play until after the next legal or illegal pitch, or until after the pitcher and all infielders have clearly vacated their normal fielding positions and have left fair territory on their way to the bench or dugout area.

h. When a batter-runner overruns first base after touching it and returns directly to the base.

i. When he is not given sufficient time to return to a base. He will not be called out for being off base before the pitcher releases the ball. "No pitch" will be called by the umpire (Rule 6, Sec. 10d (FP) and Sec. 8c (SP and 16-INCH SP).

j. When he has legally started to advance. He may not be stopped by the pitcher receiving the ball while on the pitching plate, nor by the pitcher stepping on the plate with the ball in his possession.

k. When he holds his base until a fly ball touches a fielder and then attempts to advance.

l. When hit by a batted ball when touching his base, unless he intentionally interferes with the ball or a fielder making a play.

PLAY (1) — With R1 on second, R2 on first, and no outs, B3 hits a ground ball or infield fly. Ball strikes R1 who is (a) near second, (b) standing on second. In both cases ball has not passed an infielder. RULING — In (a) R1 is out on either type of hit. In (b) R1 is not out on either type of hit, but ball becomes dead, and all runners, if forced, advance one base without liability to be put out. In both (a) and (b), B3 is out on any infield fly. If it is a ground ball, batter-runner is awarded first base.

PLAY (2) — REFER TO RULE 8, SEC. 8k.

m. When he slides into a base and dislodges it from its proper position. The base is considered to have followed the runner.

EFFECT — Sec. 9m: A baserunner reaching a base safely will not be out for being off that base if it becomes dislodged. He may return without liability to be put out when the base has been replaced. A runner forfeits this exemption if he attempts to advance beyond the dislodged base before it is again in proper position.

PLAY — R1 slides into second base. After he touches the base, he loses contact (a) because the base breaks loose from its fastening, (b) because his foot slides off the base. F4 touches him while his foot is off base. RULING — In (a) R1 is not out. In (b) R1 is out.

n. When a fielder makes a play on a batter, batter-runner, or baserunner while using an illegal glove. The manager of the offended team is given two options:

(1) He may have the entire play nullified with each baserunner returning to his original base and the batter or batter-runner batting over again, assuming the ball and strike count he had prior to the pitch he hit.

(2) He may take the result of the play and disregard the illegal act.

Sec. 10. BASERUNNING (55-Over)

a. A COURTESY RUNNER shall be allowed once per inning for any reason. The courtesy runner must be the last recorded out and must be entered prior to the first pitch to the succeeding batter. The courtesy runner is officially in the game when play ball has been declared by the umpire. An ineligible courtesy runner is an appeal situation that must be made before a legal or illegal pitch to the succeeding batter. PENALTY: The use of an ineligible courtesy runner shall result in the removal of the runner from the base and an out being recorded on the player whom he replaced.

b. A "NO SLIDE, NO CRASH" rule will be in effect at all bases, including home plate. Any and all incidents will result in an automatic out.

c. A "RUN-BY" rule shall be in effect at first, second, and third bases, (e.g., a player may run past any base at any time). The runner shall be considered "safe" so long as he turns to the right after passing the base. Any attempt to advance or to decoy the fielder cancels the "run-by" rule, and the runner may be tagged out.

NOTE: A batter-runner can turn to the right or left after overrunning first base as long as no attempt is made to advance to second base.

d. Baserunners must touch the second home plate located adjacent to the right handed batter's box in order to be safe at home. A baserunner may be retired at home plate on a non-force situation without a tag. The defensive player only has to hold the ball while touching the original home plate. If the baserunner touches the original home plate, he will be out if appealed by the defensive team.

e. Once a baserunner crosses a line 20 feet from home, he cannot return to third base. PENALTY: The baserunner will be called out if he returns.

RULE 9. DEAD BALL - BALL IN PLAY

Sec. 1. THE BALL IS DEAD AND NOT IN PLAY:

a. When a ball is batted illegally.

PLAY — R1 is on first base. B2 illegally bats the ball towards F6, and F4 obstructs R1 advancing to second base. RULING — Ball becomes dead when B2 illegally batted it. B2 is out, and R1 must return to first base.

b. When the batter steps from one box to the other when the pitcher is ready to pitch.

c. When a ball is pitched illegally.

EXCEPTION: Sec. 1c: (FP ONLY) If the pitcher completes the delivery of the ball to the batter and the batter hits the ball and reaches first base safely, and if all other baserunners advance at least one base, then the play stands, and the pitch is no longer illegal. EXCEPTION: Sec. 1c: (SP ONLY) If the batter swings at an illegal pitch, the play stands, and the pitch is no longer illegal.

d. When "NO PITCH" is declared.

e. When a pitched ball touches any part of the batter's person or clothing, whether the ball is struck at or not.

PLAY — B1 swings at a pitched ball, and the ball hits his hand while holding the bat. RULING — Strike shall be called, and the ball is dead. The hand is not considered part of the bat.

f. When a foul ball is declared.
g. When the offensive team causes the interference.
   (1) When a batter-runner intentionally strikes a fair ball a second time, strikes it with a thrown bat, or deflects its course in any way while running to first base.
   (2) When a thrown ball is intentionally touched by a coach or on-deck batter.
   (3) When a fair ball strikes a runner (not in contact with a base) or umpire before touching an infielder, including the pitcher or before passing an infielder, other than the pitcher.
   (4) When the batter interferes with the catcher or other defensive player at home plate.
   (5) When a member of the offensive team intentionally interferes with a live ball.
   (6) When a runner intentionally kicks a ball which a fielder has missed.
h. When the ball is outside the established boundaries of the playing area. A ball is considered "outside the playing field" when it touches the ground, person on the ground, or object outside the playing area.

PLAY — R1 is on third. B3 at bat with one out hits a fly ball which F5 catches in the field of play. F5's momentum causes him to go into a dead ball area such as a bench, a dugout, the stands, or the area beyond the chalk line or pre-game determined imaginary line. RULING — Ball is dead as soon as F5 enters the dead ball area with it. R1 is awarded one base, and B3 is out.

i. If an accident to a batter-runner or baserunner prevents him from proceeding to any base(s) which he is awarded. A substitute runner will be permitted for the batter-runner or baserunner and will be allowed to proceed to any awarded bas(s).

PLAY — Batter hits ball over the fence for a home run but falls down as he attempts to advance to first base. He is injured and unable to continue to play. RULING — Substitute runner will be permitted for batter-runner and will be allowed to circle the bases so that the home run may be allowed.

j. (SP ONLY) When the batter bunts or chops the pitched ball.

PLAY — REFER TO RULE 7, SEC. 11n.

k. (FP ONLY) When a wild pitch or passed ball lodges in or goes under, over, or through the backstop.
l. When time is called by the umpire.
m. When any part of the batter's person or clothing is hit with his own batted ball when he is in the batter's box.
n. When a baserunner runs bases in reverse order either to confuse the fielders or to make a travesty of the game.
o. When the batter is hit by a pitched ball.
p. When, in the judgement of the umpire, the coach near third base runs in the direction of home plate on or near the baseline while the fielder is attempting to make a play on a batted or thrown ball, and thereby draws a throw to home plate.
q. (FP ONLY) When the plate umpire or his clothing or paraphernalia interferes with the catcher's attempt to throw.
r. When one or more members of the offensive team stand or collect at or around a base to which a baserunner is advancing, thereby confusing the fielders and adding to the difficulty of making a play.
s. (FP ONLY) When a baserunner fails to keep contact with the base to which he is entitled until a legally pitched ball has been released.
t. (SP ONLY) When a baserunner fails to keep contact with the base to which he is entitled until a legally pitched ball touches the ground, reaches home plate, or is batted.
u. (SP ONLY) After each ball or strike or a pitched ball hitting the ground or plate. EXCEPTION: The ball remains alive in 16-inch slow pitch.
v. When a blocked ball is declared.
w. When a batter enters the batter's box with, or is discovered using, an altered bat.
x. When a batter enters the batter's box with, or is discovered using, an illegal bat.
y. When a caught fair fly ball, including a line drive (FP and SP) or bunt (FP ONLY), which can be handled by an infielder with ordinary effort, is intentionally dropped with fewer than two outs and a runner on first base; first and second; first and third; or first, second, and third bases.

PLAY — REFER TO RULE 7, SEC. 11h.

z. When a fielder carries a live ball into dead ball territory.
   EFFECT — Sec. 1a-z: The batter or baserunners may not advance on a dead ball unless awarded a base or bases by rule.
aa. When time has been called for a dead ball appeal.

PLAY — REFER TO RULE 8, SEC. 8i (4) AND PLAY 2.

ab. (10-Under JO Fast Pitch Only) When a pitched ball is not batted.

Sec. 2. THE BALL IS IN PLAY:
a. At the start of the game and each half inning when the pitcher has the ball while standing in his pitching position and play ball has been declared by the umpire.
b. When the infield fly rule is enforced.

PLAY — With one out, R1 is on second and R2 on first when B4 hits an infield fly. Baserunners are of the opinion two are out, and they start running as soon as the ball is hit. F4 fails to catch the infield fly, and both runners cross home plate. RULING — B4 is out for hitting infield fly, but runs count since runners may advance at their own risk.

c. When a thrown ball goes past a fielder and remains in playable territory.
d. When a fair ball strikes an umpire or baserunner on fair ground after touching an infielder, including the pitcher, or after passing an infielder, excluding the pitcher, and provided no other infielder had a chance to make an out..
e. When a fair batted ball strikes an umpire on foul ground.
f. When any runner has reached the base to which he is entitled if the fielder fields a batted or thrown ball with illegal equipment.
g. When a baserunner is called out for passing a preceding runner.

h. When a fair ball is legally batted.
i. When a baserunner must return in reverse order while the ball is in play.
j. When a batter-runner or baserunner acquires the right to a base by touching it before being put out.
k. When a base is dislodged while baserunners are progressing around the bases.
l. When a runner runs more than 3 feet (0.91 m) from a direct line between any base and the next one in regular or reverse order to avoid being touched by the ball in the hand(s) of a fielder.
m. When a runner is tagged or forced out.
n. When the umpire calls a baserunner out for failure to return and touch a base when play is resumed after a suspension of play.
o. When a live ball appeal play is legally being made.
p. When the batter legally hits the ball.
q. When a live ball strikes a photographer, groundskeeper, policeman, etc., assigned to the game.

PLAY — B1 hits a line shot which hits first base, ricochets off the bag, and hits a photographer who is assigned to take pictures of the game. Pitcher backs up play and throws out B1 advancing to second. RULING — B1 is out. Ball remains in play when it strikes a photographer who has been assigned to the game.

r. When a fair or foul fly ball has been legally caught.
s. When a thrown ball strikes an offensive player.
t. If the batter drops the bat and the ball rolls against it in fair territory and, in the judgement of the umpire, there was no intention to interfere with the course of the ball. The batter-runner is not out, and the ball is alive and in play.
u. When a thrown ball strikes an umpire.
v. When a play is or is not being made on an obstructed runner, or if the batter-runner is obstructed before he touches first base.
w. When a thrown ball strikes a coach.
x. (FP and 16-INCH SP ONLY) When a ball has been called on the batter. When four balls have been called, the batter may not be put out before he reaches first base.
y. (FP and 16-INCH SP ONLY) When a strike has been called on the batter.
z. (FP and 16-INCH SP ONLY) When a foul tip has been legally caught.

PLAY — Does the ball become dead after a foul tip, and may there be a foul tip which is not caught? RULING — The ball does not become dead on a foul tip. On a foul tip and a runner may advance or be put out the same as after any strike. To be a foul tip, the ball must be caught by the catcher.

aa. (SP ONLY) As long as there is a play as a result of a hit by the batter-runner. This includes a subsequent appeal play.
ab. (FP and 16-INCH SP ONLY) If the ball slips from a pitcher's hand during his windup or the backswing.
ac. Whenever the ball is not dead, as provided in Sec. 1 of this rule.

Sec. 3. DELAYED DEAD BALL. There are six situations when a violation of the rule occurs, it is recognized by an umpire, and the ball remains live until the conclusion of the play. These situations are:
a. An illegal pitch (Rule 6, Sections 1-8)
b. Catcher's obstruction (Rule 8, Section 6d)
c. Plate umpire interference (Rule 8, Section 6d)
d. Obstruction (Rule 8, Section 5b)
e. Batted or thrown ball hit with detached equipment (Rule 8, Section 5f)
f. Runner at third or first base assisted by a coach on a tag up (Rule 8, Section 8m)
NOTE: Once the entire play is completed in each situation, the proper enforcement should be made. In (e), a double play could be called. One out on the coach assisting the runner and the second out on the caught ball.

Sec. 4. (SP ONLY) THE BALL REMAINS ALIVE UNTIL THE UMPIRE CALLS TIME, WHICH SHOULD BE DONE WHEN THE BALL IS HELD BY A PLAYER IN THE INFIELD AREA AND, IN THE JUDGEMENT OF THE UMPIRE, ALL PLAY HAS CEASED.

RULE 10. UMPIRES

NOTE: Failure of umpires to adhere to Rule 10 shall not be grounds for protest. These are guidelines for umpires.

Sec. 1. POWER AND DUTIES. The umpires are the representatives of the league or organization by which they have been assigned to a particular game and, as such, are authorized and required to enforce each section of these rules. They have the power to order a player, coach, captain, or manager to carry out or to omit any act which, in their judgement, is necessary to give force and effect to one or all of these rules, and to inflict penalties as herein prescribed. The plate umpire shall have the authority to make decisions on any situations not specifically covered in the rules. THE FOLLOWING IS THE GENERAL INFORMATION FOR UMPIRES:
a. The umpire will not be a member of either team (i.e., player, coach, manager, officer, scorer, or sponsor).
b. The umpire should be sure of the date, time, and place of the game and should arrive at the playing field 20-30 minutes ahead of time, start the game at the designated time, and leave the field when the game is over. His jurisdiction begins when he enters the field to check the bats and ends when he leaves the field following the completion of the game.
c. The male and female umpire shall wear a powder blue, short-sleeve shirt; dark navy blue slacks; and a cap with white ASA letters on the front. All other paraphernalia (i.e., socks, ball bag, jacket, and/or sweater) must also be dark navy blue, and the shoes and belt must be black for both male and female umpires. A t-shirt is optional to wear under the powder blue shirt; however, if one is worn, it must be white. The plate umpire in fast pitch MUST wear a black mask with a black throat protector. (An extended wire protector may be worn in lieu of a throat protector on the mask.) Body protectors are recommended for umpires in fast pitch and are optional in slow pitch.
d. The umpires should introduce themselves to the captains, managers, and scorers.

e. The umpires should inspect the playing field boundaries and equipment and clarify all ground rules for the representatives of both teams.
f. Each umpire will have the power to make decisions on violations committed anytime during playing time or during suspension of play.
g. No umpire has the authority to set aside or question decisions made by another umpire within the limits of his respective duties as outlined in these rules.
h. An umpire may consult his associate(s) at any time; however, the final decision will rest with the umpire whose exclusive authority it is to make the decision and who requests the opinion of the other umpire(s).
i. In order to define "respective duties," the umpire whose primary responsibility is the judging of balls and strikes will be designated as the PLATE UMPIRE, while the umpire whose primary responsibility is the rendering of base decisions will be designated as the BASE UMPIRE.
j. The plate umpire and base umpire will have equal authority to:
   (1) Call a runner out for leaving a base too soon.
   (2) Call TIME for suspension of play.
   (3) Eject a player, coach, manager, or other team member from the game for violation of rules or flagrant misconduct.
   (4) Call all illegal pitches.
k. The umpire will declare the batter or runner out, without waiting for an appeal for such decision, in all cases where such player is retired in accordance with these rules.

NOTE: Unless appealed to, the umpire will not call a player out for failure to touch a base, for leaving a base too soon on a caught fly ball, for batting out of order, or for making an attempt to go to second after reaching first base, as provided in these rules.

l. The umpire will not penalize a team for infraction of a rule when imposing the penalty would be to the advantage of the offending team.

Sec. 2. THE PLATE UMPIRE SHOULD:

a. Take a position behind the catcher. He will have full charge of and be responsible for the proper conduct of the game.
b. Call all balls and strikes, unless he requests the help of another umpire.
c. By agreement and in cooperation with the base umpire, makes decisions on plays, fair or foul balls, and legally or illegally caught balls. On plays which would necessitate the base umpire leaving the infield in a two umpire system, the plate umpire will assume the duties normally required of the base umpire.
d. Determine and declare whether:
   (1) A batter bunts or chops a ball.
   (2) A batted ball touches the person or clothing of the batter.
   (3) A fly ball is an infield or an outfield fly.
e. Render base decisions as indicated in the *Umpire's Manual*.
f. Determine when a game is forfeited.
g. Assume all duties when assigned as a single umpire to a game.

Sec. 3. THE BASE UMPIRE SHOULD:

a. Take such positions on the playing field as outlined in the *Umpire's Manual*.
b. Assist the plate umpire in every way to enforce the rules of the game.

Sec. 4. RESPONSIBILITIES OF A SINGLE UMPIRE. If only one umpire is assigned, his duties and jurisdictions will extend to all points. The umpire's starting position for each pitch should be from behind home plate. On each batted ball or play that develops, the umpire must move out from behind the plate and into the infield to obtain the best position for any play that develops.

Sec. 5. CHANGE OF UMPIRES. Teams may not request a change of umpires during a game unless an umpire is incapacitated by injury or illness.

Sec. 6. UMPIRE'S JUDGEMENT. There will be no appeal on any decision of any umpire on the grounds that he was not correct in his conclusion as to whether a batted ball was fair or foul, a runner safe or out, a pitched ball a ball or strike, or on any play involving accuracy of judgement; and no decision rendered by any umpire will be reversed except when he is convinced it is in violation of one of these rules. In case the manager, acting manager, or captain of either team does seek reversal of a decision based solely on a point of rules, the umpire whose decision is in question will, if in doubt, confer with his associate(s) before taking any action; but under no circumstances will any player or person, other than the manager, acting manager, or captain of either team, have any legal right to protest any decision and seek its reversal on a claim that it is in conflict with these rules.

a. Under no circumstances will any umpire seek to reverse a decision made by an associate, nor will any umpire criticize or interfere with the duties of his associate(s) unless asked to do so.
b. The umpire-in-chief may rectify any situation in which the reversal of an umpire's decision or a delayed call by an umpire places a batter-runner, a baserunner, or the defensive team in jeopardy. This correction is not possible after one legal or illegal pitch has been thrown, or after the pitcher and all infielders have clearly vacated their normal fielding positions and have left fair territory on their way to the bench or dugout area.

PLAY — With R1 on first base and fewer than two outs, the runner attempts to steal second on the pitch (FP ONLY). The catcher throws to second base as the plate umpire calls ball four. The throw is in time, and the base umpire calls the runner out. As the runner (R1) leaves for the dugout, the base umpire realizes B2 has four balls and R1 is entitled to second base. The defense tags R1 when he leaves the base. Had the umpire not called R1 out, he would not have left the base. RULING — Place R1 on second base and B2 on first base.

Sec. 7. SIGNALS:

a. **SAFE** — Body upright, eyes on the ball, and arms extended straight out with the palms down. A verbal call of "SAFE" is made as the arms are snapped to this position from the upper chest.
b. **SAFE SELL** — The same as the safe call, but as the arms are extended straight out with the palms down, a step should be taken towards the play.
c. **OUT** — Body upright, eyes on the ball, and right arm extended straight up as an extension of the shoulder. As we come to the HAMMER position, the elbow is bent at a 90° angle and the fist closed with the fingers facing the right ear. The left arm should be brought to the mid-section of the body. A verbal call of "OUT" is made as the right arm is extended high into the air and continued as the arm drops into the HAMMER position.
d. **OUT SELL** — Come to upright position and take a step with left foot directly at the play. Your head should remain in position looking at the play as the upper torso turns perpendicularly from the play. Raise right arm with an open hand behind your head into a throwing position as you shuffle your right foot behind the left. Plant right foot and transfer weight, bringing right arm over the top of your head with a closed fist, and make a vigorous OUT call. Finish call by transferring your weight to the left foot while bringing the right foot forward and parallel to the left.
e. **STRIKE** — Body upright, eyes on the ball, and right arm extended straight up as an extension of the shoulder. As we come to the HAMMER position, the elbow is bent at a 90° angle, and the fist is closed with the fingers facing the right ear. The left arm should be brought to the mid-section of the body. A verbal call of "STRIKE" is made as the right arm is extended high into the air and continued as the arm drops into the HAMMER position.
f. **FAIR BALL** — Body upright, eyes on the ball, and point toward fair territory with the arm that is toward the infield. There is no verbal call on a fair ball, and if the umpire is wearing a mask, it should be in the left hand.
g. **FOUL BALL** — On all foul balls except a caught foul fly ball, the ball is DEAD, and the DEAD BALL signal should be given preceding the foul ball signal. For the FOUL BALL signal, body should be upright, eyes on the ball, and the arm extended straight out from the shoulder toward foul territory away from the playing field. A verbal call of "FOUL BALL" should be declared as the arm motion is made.
h. **TIME OUT/DEAD BALL** — Body upright, and both arms extended high into the air with the palms of the hands open and facing away from the umpire's body. A verbal call of "TIME" or "DEAD BALL" is made at the same time the arms are going up.
i. **PLAY BALL** — Body upright, eyes on the ball, and the umpire makes a motion toward the pitcher with the right or left hand. On a right handed batter use the right hand, and on a left-handed batter use the left hand. A verbal call of "PLAY" or "PLAY BALL" is made as the umpire motions toward the pitcher.
j. **HOLD UP PLAY** (No Pitch) — Body upright, and raise either hand with the palm facing the pitcher. On a right-handed batter use the right hand, and on a left-handed batter use the left hand. "NO PITCH" shall be declared if the pitcher pitches while the umpire has a hand in said position.
k. **DELAYED DEAD BALL** — Body upright. The left arm is extended straight out to the side of the body as an extension of the shoulder, and the left hand is in a fist. This position is held long enough for the players to see that the umpire has observed the act that pre-empted this call.
l. **INFIELD FLY** — Body upright, eyes on the ball, and right arm extended high into the air with a closed fist. Make a verbal call of "INFIELD FLY." If the batted ball is near a foul line, call "INFIELD FLY IF FAIR."
m. **TRAPPED BALL** — Same as safe signal. The umpire makes a verbal call of "SAFE."
n. **FOUL TIP** — Body upright and eyes on the ball. The fingers of both hands are touched together, and then the umpire gives the strike signal with no verbal call. This indicates that the bat tipped the ball and was caught by the catcher.
o. **COUNT** — Body upright. Have eye contact with the pitcher. Both hands are extended high above the head, and the fingers are used to indicate the ball and strike count on the batter. Use the fingers of the left hand for balls and the fingers of the right hand for strikes. A verbal description of the count on the batter is given while the hands are overhead. Balls are always mentioned first and strikes second.
p. **DOUBLE** — Body upright. Raise the right hand high above the head, indicating with two fingers the number of bases awarded. A verbal call of "TWO BASES" is made while the hand remains overhead.
q. **HOME RUN** — Body upright. Raise the right hand high above the head with a closed fist. Make a counter-clockwise circling motion with the raised fist. A verbal call of "FOUR BASES" is made at the same time the fist is overhead.
r. **FOUR-BASE AWARD** — Body upright. Raise the right hand high above the head with four fingers shown. A verbal call of "FOUR-BASE AWARD" is made at the same time the hand is overhead.

Sec. 8. SUSPENSION OF PLAY:

a. An umpire may suspend play when, in his judgement, conditions justify such action.
b. Play will be suspended whenever the plate umpire leaves his position to brush the plate or to perform other duties not directly connected with the calling of plays.
c. The umpire will suspend play whenever a batter or pitcher steps out of position for a legitimate reason.
d. An umpire will not call time after pitcher has started his windup.
e. An umpire will not call time while any play is in progress.
f. In case of injury, time will not be called until all plays in progress have been completed or each runner has been held at his base.
g. Umpires will not suspend play at the request of players, coaches, or managers until all action in progress by either team has been completed.

PLAY — Bases are full. B4 hits a long fly to center. F7 and F8 collide in trying to make the catch, and both are injured. All runners cross home plate. Captain requests time to prevent the last two runs from scoring. RULING — Ball does not become dead when a player is injured during a batted, pitched (FP), or thrown ball. Umpire will not call time until no further play is possible. All four runs count.

h. (SP ONLY) When, in the judgement of an umpire, all immediate play is apparently completed, he should call time.

Sec. 9. VIOLATIONS AND PENALTIES:

a. Players, coaches, managers, or other team members will not make disparaging or insulting remarks to or about opposing players, officials, or spectators; or commit other acts that could be considered unsportsmanlike conduct.
b. There will be no more than two coaches for each team to give words or signals of assistance and direction to the members of their team while at bat. One should be stationed near first base and the other near third base. Each coach must remain in his coach's box.
c. The penalty for violations by a player is prompt removal of the offender from the game and grounds. For the first offense, a coach or manager may be warned, but for the second offense, he is removed from the game. The offender should go directly to the dressing room or leave the grounds for the remainder of the game. Failure to do so will warrant a forfeiture of the game.

RULE 11. PROTESTS

Sec. 1. PROTESTS WILL NOT BE RECEIVED OR CONSIDERED IF THEY ARE BASED SOLELY ON A DECISION INVOLVING THE ACCURACY OF JUDGEMENT ON THE PART OF AN UMPIRE. Examples of protests which will not be considered are:

a. Whether a batted ball was fair or foul.

b. Whether a runner was safe or out.

c. Whether a pitched ball was a ball or a strike.

d. Whether a pitch was legal or illegal.

e. Whether a runner did or did not touch a base.

f. Whether a baserunner did or did not leave his base too soon on a caught fly ball.

g. Whether a fly ball was or was not caught legally.

h. Whether it was or was not an infield fly.

i. Whether there was or was not interference or obstruction.

j. Whether the field is or is not fit to continue or resume play.

k. Whether there is or is not sufficient light to continue play.

l. Any other matter involving only the accuracy of the umpire's judgement.

m. Whether a batted ball did or did not clear the fence in flight.

n. Whether a batted ball was or was not touched by a fielder before clearing the fence in flight.

o. Whether a player or live ball did or did not enter a dead ball area or touch some object or person in a dead ball area.

Sec. 2. PROTESTS THAT SHALL BE RECEIVED AND CONSIDERED CONCERN MATTERS OF THE FOLLOWING TYPES:

a. Misinterpretation of a playing rule.

b. Failure of an umpire to apply the correct rule to a given situation.

c. Failure of an umpire to impose the correct penalty for a given violation.

Sec. 3. PROTESTS MAY INVOLVE BOTH A MATTER OF JUDGEMENT AND THE INTERPRETATION OF A RULE.

EXAMPLE:

With one out and runners on second and third, the batter flies out. The runner on third tags up after the catch, but the runner on second does not. The runner on third crosses the plate before the ball is played at second base for the third out. The umpire does not allow the run to score. The questions as to whether the runners left their bases before the catch or whether the play at second base was made before the runner on third crossed the plate are solely matters of judgement and are not protestable. It is a misinterpretation of a playing rule and a proper subject for protest, however, if the umpire fails to allow the run to score.

Sec. 4. THE NOTIFICATION OF INTENT TO PROTEST MUST BE MADE IMMEDIATELY BEFORE THE NEXT LEGAL OR ILLEGAL PITCH OR BEFORE BOTH TEAMS HAVE LEFT THE PLAYING FIELD. (EXCEPTION: Player eligibility)

PLAY (1) — R1 is obstructed by F4 while advancing to second during a rundown between first and second bases. Umpire rules OBSTRUCTION and returns R1 to first base. Offensive team protests game (a) before first pitch to B2, (b) after first pitch to B2, (c) after game is over. RULING — In (a) protest is valid. In (b) and (c) protest is denied since it was not made before the next pitch.

PLAY (2) — Bases loaded, bottom of seventh inning, two outs, and the score is visitors 4, home 3. Home team (offensive) coach calls a second conference with a batter in that half inning. The plate umpire calls the batter out to end the game. Both teams are off the playing field and preparing to leave when the home manager protests to the umpire in the parking lot that the ruling was incorrect. RULING — The game is over. When both teams have left the playing field, no protest may be accepted.

a. The manager, acting manager, or captain of the protesting team shall immediately notify the plate umpire that the game is being played under protest. The plate umpire shall in turn notify the opposing manager and official scorekeeper.

b. To aid in the correct determination of the issue, all interested parties shall take notice of the information, details, and conditions surrounding the decision to protest.

NOTE: On appeal plays, the appeal must be made before the next pitch, legal or illegal, or before the defensive team has left the field. For the purpose of this rule, the defensive team has "left the field" when the pitcher and all infielders have clearly vacated their normal fielding positions and have left fair territory on their way to the bench or dugout area.

c. Once the game is completed and both teams have left the field, no protest may be filed. EXCEPTION: Player eligibility.

Sec. 5. THE OFFICIAL WRITTEN PROTEST MUST BE FILED WITHIN A REASONABLE TIME:

a. In the absence of a league or tournament rule establishing the time limit for filing a protest, a protest should be considered if filed within a reasonable time, depending upon the nature of the case and the difficulty of obtaining the information relevant to the protest.

b. Within 48 hours after the scheduled time of the contest is generally considered a reasonable time.

Sec. 6. THE FOLLOWING WRITTEN PROTEST SHOULD CONTAIN THE FOLLOWING INFORMATION:

a. The date, time, and place of the game.

b. The names of the umpires and scorers.

c. The rule and section of the official rules or local rules under which the protest is made.

d. The information, details, and conditions pertinent to the decision to protest.

e. All essential facts involved in the matter protested.

Sec. 7. THE DECISION RENDERED ON A PROTESTED GAME MUST RESULT IN ONE OF THE FOLLOWING:

a. The protest is determined to be invalid, and the game score stands as played.

b. When a protest is determined to be valid because of the misinterpretation of a playing rule, the decision will be corrected, and the game shall be replayed from the point at which the incorrect decision was made.

c. When a protest for ineligibility is determined to be valid, the offending team shall forfeit the game being played, or the game last played, to the offended team.

RULE 12. SCORING

NOTE: Failure of official scorer to adhere to Rule 12 shall not be grounds for protest. These are guidelines for the official scorer.

Sec. 1. THE OFFICIAL SCORER SHALL KEEP RECORDS OF EACH GAME AS OUTLINED IN THE FOLLOWING RULES. He shall have sole authority to make all decisions involving judgement. For example, it is the scorer's responsibility to determine whether a batter-runner's advance to first base is the result of a hit or an error; however, a scorer shall not make a decision which conflicts with the official playing rules or with an umpire's decision.

Sec. 2. THE BOX SCORE:

a. Each player's name and the position or positions he has played shall be listed in the order in which he batted or would have batted had he not been removed or had the game not ended before his turn at bat.

  (1) (FP ONLY) The designated player (DP) is optional, but if one is used, it must be made known prior to the start of the game and listed on the scoresheet in the regular batting order. Ten names will be listed, with the tenth name being the player playing defense only. This tenth player may only bat if he moves to the DP position in the batting order.

EXCEPTION: See Rule 4, Sec. 3c.

  (2) (SP ONLY) The extra player (EP) is optional, but if one is used, it must be made known prior to the start of the game and listed on the scoring sheet in the regular batting order. There will be 11 names for men's and women's slow pitch and 12 names for co-ed slow pitch on the official batting order, and all will bat.

b. Each player's batting and fielding record must be tabulated.

  (1) The first column will show the number of times at bat by each player, but a time at bat will not be charged against the player when:

    (a) He hits a sacrifice fly that scores a runner.

    (b) He is awarded a base on balls.

    (c) (FP ONLY) He hits a sacrifice bunt.

    (d) (FP ONLY) He is hit by a pitched ball.

    (e) (FP ONLY) He hits a sacrifice slap hit. NOTE: A *slap hit* is defined as "a fake bunt followed by a controlled swing and resulting in the baserunner(s) advancing," as in the case of a sacrifice bunt.

  (2) The second column will show the number of runs scored by each player.

  (3) The third column will show the number of base hits made by each player. A base hit is a batted ball that permits the batter to reach base safely:

    (a) On a fair ball which settles on the ground, clears the fence, or strikes the fence before being touched by a fielder.

    (b) On a fair ball which is hit with such force or such slowness, or which takes such an unnatural bounce, that it is impossible to field with ordinary effort in time to retire the runner.

    (c) When a fair ball which has not been touched by a fielder becomes dead because of touching the person or clothing of a runner or umpire.

    (d) When a fielder unsuccessfully attempts to retire a preceding runner and, in the scorer's judgement, the batter-runner would not have been retired at first base by perfect fielding.

  (4) The fourth column will show the number of opponents put out by each player.

    (a) A putout is credited to a fielder each time he:

      (1) Catches a fly ball or line drive.

      (2) Catches a thrown ball which retires a batter-runner or baserunner.

      (3) Touches a baserunner with ball when the baserunner is off the base to which he is entitled.

      (4) Is nearest the ball when a runner is declared out for being struck by a fair batted ball or for interference with a fielder, or when a runner is called out for being in violation of Rule 8, Sec. 8e and Sec. 8u.

    (b) A putout is credited to the catcher:

      (1) When a third strike is called.

      (2) (SP ONLY) When the batter bunts or chops the ball downward.

      (3) When the batter fails to bat in correct order.

      (4) When the batter interferes with the catcher.

      (5) (SP ONLY) When the batter hits a third strike foul ball.

  (5) The fifth column shall show the number of assists made by each player. An assist shall be credited:

    (a) To each player who handles the ball in any series of plays which results in the putout of a baserunner or batter-runner. Only one assist shall be given to any player who handles the ball on any putout. The player who makes the putout in a rundown or similar-type play shall be credited with both an assist and a putout.

    (b) To each player who handles or throws the ball in such a manner that a putout would have resulted except for an error of a teammate.

    (c) To each player who, by deflecting a batted ball, aids in a putout.

    (d) To each player who handles the ball on a play which results in a baserunner or batter-runner being called out for interference or for running out of the baseline.

  (6) The sixth column will show the number of errors made by each player. Errors are recorded:

    (a) For each player who commits a misplay which prolongs the turn at bat of the batter or the life of a present runner.

    (b) For the fielder who fails to touch a base after receiving a thrown ball to retire a runner on a force out, or when a baserunner is compelled to return to a base, and provided the thrown ball could be caught by the fielder with ordinary effort.

    (c) For the catcher if a batter is awarded first base because of catcher obstruction.

    (d) For the fielder who fails to complete a double play because of a dropped ball.

    (e) For a fielder, if a runner advances a base because of said fielder's failure to catch, stop, or try to stop a ball accurately thrown to a base, provided there was occasion for the throw. When more than one player could receive the throw, the scorer must determine which player gets the error.

Sec. 3. A BASE HIT SHALL NOT BE SCORED:

a. When a runner is forced out on a batted ball or would have been forced out **except** for a fielding error.

b. When a player fielding a batted ball retires a preceding runner with ordinary effort.

c. When a fielder fails in an attempt to retire a preceding runner and, in the scorer's judgement, the batter-runner could have been retired at first base.

Sec. 4. A RUN BATTED IN IS A RUN SCORED BECAUSE OF:

a. A safe hit.
b. A sacrifice bunt (FP), a sacrifice slap hit (FP), or a sacrifice fly (FP and SP). See Rule 1, Sec. 55)
c. A caught foul fly.
d. An infield putout or fielder's choice.
e. A baserunner forced home because of obstruction, a hit batsman, or a base on balls.
f. A home run and all runs scored as a result.

Sec. 5. A PITCHER SHALL BE CREDITED WITH A WIN:

a. When he is the starting pitcher, has pitched at least four innings, and his team is not only in the lead when he is replaced, but remains in the lead for the remainder of the game.
b. When a starting pitcher has pitched at least three innings and his team scores more runs than the opposing team in a game that is terminated after five innings of play, or in a game that is terminated after his team has scored more runs in four or more innings than the opposing team has scored in five or more innings; and provided that his team is not only in the lead if he is replaced after three innings of pitching, but remains in the lead for the remainder of the game.

Sec. 6. REGARDLESS OF THE NUMBER OF INNINGS HE HAS PITCHED, A PITCHER SHALL BE CHARGED WITH A LOSS IF HE IS REPLACED WHEN HIS TEAM IS BEHIND IN THE SCORE AND FAILS TO TIE THE SCORE OR GAIN THE LEAD THEREAFTER.

Sec. 7: THE SUMMARY SHALL LIST THE FOLLOWING ITEMS IN THIS ORDER:

a. The score by innings and the final score.
b. The runs batted in and by whom.
c. Two-base hits and by whom.
d. Three-base hits and by whom.
e. Home runs and by whom.
f. Sacrifice flies and by whom.
g. Double plays and players participating in them.
h. Triple plays and players participating in them.
i. Number of bases on balls charged to each pitcher.
j. Number of batters struck out by each pitcher.
k. Number of hits and runs allowed by each pitcher.
l. The name of the winning pitcher.
m. The name of the losing pitcher.
n. The time of the game.
o. The names of the umpires and scorers.
p. (FP ONLY) Stolen bases and by whom.
q. (FP ONLY) Sacrifice bunts and by whom.
r. (FP ONLY) The names of batters hit by a pitched ball and the names of the pitchers who hit them.
s. (FP ONLY) The number of wild pitches charged to each pitcher.
t. (FP ONLY) The number of passed balls charged to each catcher.

Sec. 8. (FP ONLY) A STOLEN BASE IS CREDITED TO A BASERUNNER WHENEVER HE ADVANCES ONE BASE UNAIDED BY A HIT, PUTOUT, FORCE OUT, FIELDER'S CHOICE, PASSED BALL, WILD PITCH, AN ERROR, AN ILLEGAL PITCH, OR OBSTRUCTION.

Sec. 9. ALL RECORDS OF A FORFEITED GAME WILL BE INCLUDED IN THE OFFICIAL RECORDS EXCEPT THAT OF A PITCHER'S WON-LOST RECORD.

Ordering *Sports Rules in Pictures* and *Sports Tecniques in Pictures* is easy and convenient. Just call 1-800-631-8571 or send your order to:

The Putnam Publishing Group
390 Murray Hill Parkway, Dept. B
East Rutherford, NJ 07073
Also available at your local bookstore or wherever paperbacks are sold.

			US	CANADA
_____	Baseball Rules in Pictures	399-51597	$7.95	$10.50
_____	Official Little League	399-51531	$7.95	$10.50
	Baseball Rules in Pictures			
_____	Softball Rules in Pictures	399-51728	$7.95	$10.50
_____	Football Rules in Pictures	399-51689	$7.95	$10.50
_____	Basketball Rules in Pictures	399-51590	$7.95	$10.50
_____	Hockey Rules in Pictures	399-51480	$7.95	$10.50
_____	Amateur Wrestling Rules in Pictures	399-51589	$7.95	$10.50
_____	Volleyball Rules in Pictures	399-51537	$7.95	$10.50
_____	Golf Rules in Pictures	399-51438	$7.95	$10.50
_____	Tennis Rules and Techniques in Pictures	399-51674	$7.95	$10.50
_____	Track and Field Rules in Pictures	399-51620	$7.95	$10.50
_____	Gymnastics Rules in Pictures	399-51636	$7.95	$10.50
_____	Soccer Rules in Pictures	399-51647	$7.95	$10.50
_____	Golf Techniques in Pictures	399-51664	$7.95	$10.50
_____	Soccer Techniques in Pictures	399-51701	$7.95	$10.50

Subtotal $ _____
*Postage & Handling $ _____
Sales Tax $ _____
(CA, NJ, NY, PA)
Total Amount Due $ _____
Payable in U.S. Funds
(No cash orders accepted)
$10.00 minimum for credit card orders.

*Postage & Handling: $2.00 for 1 book, $.50 for each additional book up to a maximum of $4.50.

Please send me the titles checked above. Enclosed is my:

❑ check   ❑ money order

Please charge my:

❑ Visa   ❑ MasterCard   ❑ American Express

Card # _____ Expiration date _____

Signature as on charge card _____

Name _____

Address _____

City _____ State _____ Zip _____

Please allow six weeks for delivery. Prices subject to change without notice.